THE
SELF-MOTIVATION
MINDSET
JOURNAL FOR MEN

A 7-STEP GUIDE FOR
SELF-IMPROVEMENT

By Heath Dixon

CONTENTS

INTRODUCTION   **1**

CHAPTER 1   **7**
DISCOVER YOUR TRUE PASSIONS   7

CHAPTER 2   **29**
SET MEANINGFUL GOALS   29

CHAPTER 3   **57**
CULTIVATE A GROWTH MINDSET   57
    The Mindsets Theory   58
    10 Steps to Develop a Growth Mindset   67

BE A CATALYST!   **75**

CHAPTER 4   **77**
OVERCOME PROCRASTINATION AND PERFECTIONISM   77
    Understanding Procrastination and Perfectionism   78
    When perfectionism and procrastination go too far: Analysis paralysis   89
    Taking lessons from failure   93

CHAPTER 5   **97**
BUILD RESILIENCE AND MENTAL TOUGHNESS   97
    External Adversities: An Unpredictable Terrain   98
    The Chaos Out There: Embracing the Limits of Control   103
    The Art of Responding, Not Reacting   108

CHAPTER 6   **113**

SURROUND YOURSELF WITH SUPPORTIVE RELATIONSHIPS   113

   Building a Network of Supportive Relationships   115

   The advantages of surrounding yourself with positive influences   120

   How do we build supportive relationships?   123

   Different types of supportive relationships: Mentors 126

CHAPTER 7   **133**

EMBRACE LIFELONG LEARNING WITH MINDFULNESS   133

   Understanding Lifelong Learning   135

   The Synergy between Mindfulness and Lifelong Growth 141

   Mindful Growth   146

   Self-Reflection and Alignment in Lifelong Growth   147

INSPIRE ANOTHER READER!   **153**

CONCLUSION   **155**

REFERENCES   **159**

YOUR FREE BONUS

Included with your purchase of this book is *Punctuality's Playbook*. This blueprint offers the tools to help you master time, crush deadlines, and transform into a punctual powerhouse.

Click the below link or scan the QR code and let us know what email address to deliver it to.

https://hdixonpublishing.com/punctualitysplaybook

If you have any issues, disable your browser's adblocker for this page.

INTRODUCTION

"The only person you are destined to become is the person you decide to be."

- Ralph Waldo Emerson

When I was a kid, reading wasn't exactly my favorite pastime, but there was one series in our family's book collection that I couldn't resist. Known as the "Choose Your Own Adventure" series, it was a childhood favorite of mine.

If you have not heard of these books, they have a unique quality that makes them stand out. Unlike traditional books, where the plot is fixed and unalterable, these books let you decide how the story will unfold.

Imagine me as an eight-year-old curled up on the couch with my nose buried in a book. With every page turned, I found myself confronted with choices, each carrying the power to transform the narrative, leading me down diverse and uncharted paths. I wasn't merely reading a story but actively creating it with my decisions.

These early reading adventures sparked my curiosity, planting the seeds for a lifelong fascination with the power of choices. Fast-forwarding to my adult years, curiosity has remained one of my primary positive traits, almost a lens through which I view the world.

What if I told you that life is the ultimate "Choose Your Own Adventure" story? In life's journey, every day is a new chapter, every choice a pivotal moment, and every opportunity a hidden twist in the plot. **Ultimately, your decisions are the ink that writes the story of your own epic tale.**

Just like those beloved childhood books, life holds endless possibilities. Each choice you make, whether monumental or insignificant, leads to a different path, crafting a unique narrative that is exclusively yours. Your decisions shape your reality, reflecting the profound fact that you are the architect of your destiny. The importance of this point is often overlooked, which is why most people live their lives as if they were going through the motions.

Within these pages, we'll uncover the secrets to building a meaningful life, guided by the same wonder and curiosity that once captivated my eight-year-old self while reading on the couch.

Taking this journey is not about perfection; it's about progress. It's about taking one step at a time, learning from every setback, and forging ahead with determination and purpose. If you're willing to commit to your growth and rekindle the flame of self-motivation, you're in the right place.

Years ago, I stood at a crossroads, much like the ones I encountered in the books of my childhood. This time, however, the choice I faced would significantly impact my life. A dilemma arose: whether to embark on an entrepreneurial adventure by starting my own business or to remain in my familiar job. Like any decision that pushes you beyond your comfort zone, the potential for great success was there, but so were the risks of failure. It wasn't a simple choice; I had to weigh the consequences meticulously, pondering how they might impact my career path and life's journey.

Ultimately, I decided to jump into the world of entrepreneurship, a move that changed everything for the better. As I reflect, it was a decision I could take because I believed in my abilities. That choice was hard, but I was confident I could make something great.

A couple of years after taking that leap into entrepreneurship and reaping its rewards, I took the time to reflect on the steps that led me to success. I jotted down my thoughts on paper. Today, that paper has become the book you're holding.

In today's fast-paced and competitive world, we must harness our inner motivation and strive for personal growth. Who hasn't struggled with self-motivation, stuck in a rut, lacking the drive to pursue their goals and dreams? If you're ready to break free from these limitations and unlock your true potential, "The Self-Motivation Mindset Journal" is the right guide.

You're holding the result of my journey of self-discovery and personal growth. I have faced and overcome many of the same challenges you're experiencing. I understand the pain of feeling stuck, the frustration of unfulfilled dreams, and the yearning for self-motivation. My personal and professional experiences have given me the insights and strategies to help you become your best self.

Before we delve into the seven steps that will transform your life, let's take a moment to acknowledge the challenges you've been facing. It's essential to recognize that you're not alone in your struggles. In today's world, where the pace of life is relentless and the expectations are high, we all find ourselves grappling with the same issues.

The daily routine can be exhausting. The pressures of work, family, and social expectations can leave you feeling overwhelmed and drained. **It's easy to lose sight of your dreams when constantly juggling responsibilities and battling the fatigue that accompanies a busy life.**

Even if you had your goals in mind, you may have encountered setbacks along the way: failed endeavors, missed opportunities, or moments of self-doubt. These experiences can undermine your self-motivation, making it harder to summon the energy to pursue your goals.

Remember this: Every challenge you've faced, every setback you've endured, has brought you to this moment. This is all part of your journey. You can learn to draw strength from these experiences to reignite your self-motivation mindset and shape your future.

My aim is not to provide you with a quick fix or a magical formula for success. Instead, I offer you deep insight into understanding the human spirit, motivation, and resilience. "The Self-Motivation Mindset Journal" is not just another self-help book. It's a comprehensive roadmap designed to empower you to take control of your life. By combining my personal experience with evidence-based theories from diverse disciplines such as psychology and sociology, this book offers a simplified 7-step guide to gaining control over your future.

Step by step, we will delve into the art of cultivating self-motivation, conquering obstacles, and shaping a destiny that resonates with your true aspirations. By the time you reach the final page, you will have the tools, strategies, and insights needed to:

- **Cultivate Unshakable Self-Motivation:** You'll learn how to reignite your inner fire and maintain self-motivation by harnessing the power of your true passions.
- **Set and Achieve Your Goals:** Discover how to set clear, inspiring goals and develop a roadmap to turn your dreams into reality.
- **Master Your Mind:** Understand the power of your thoughts and emotions and learn to cultivate a growth mindset.
- **Overcome Procrastination:** Gain the skills to conquer the inner obstacles that have held you back.
- **Build Resilience:** Strengthen your ability to recover from setbacks and cultivate the mental toughness needed to endure challenges along your path.
- **Enhance Relationships:** Strengthen your connections with others and build a support system that empowers your journey.
- **Embrace Mindful Lifelong Learning:** Discover how to sail through the vast sea of knowledge using mindfulness as your guide, ensuring your journey toward self-improvement is always enlightening.

Ultimately, "The Self-Motivation Mindset Journal" will guide you to a life of purpose, fulfillment, and personal growth, where you wake up each day with enthusiasm for what lies ahead.

In the following chapters, we will explore each of the seven steps in detail, providing practical exercises, real-life examples, and actionable strategies. The path to personal growth and self-improvement begins now, and "The Self-Motivation Mindset Journal" is your trusted companion on this remarkable journey. So, are you ready to take that first step toward your brighter future? Let's dive in.

DECLARATION OF INTENT

I,_____, commit myself to the profound journey of self-discovery and growth that lies within the pages of this book.

With an open heart and sincere intentions, I commit to embracing both the light and shadows of my being, seeking healing and self-reflection.

With this declaration, I embark on a journey of self-discovery, knowing that every word absorbed, every page turned, and every insight gained will contribute to my personal growth and enlightenment.

_____

[Your Name]

_____

[Date]

DISCOVER YOUR TRUE PASSIONS

"Passion is energy. Feel the power that comes from focusing on what excites you."

- Oprah Winfrey

Throughout history, the world has witnessed the rise of extraordinary personalities who made an impact on society. Think of visionaries like Leonardo da Vinci, pioneers like Marie Curie, or innovators like Steve Jobs. You probably marvel at their achievements and wonder how they reached such heights of success. What was their secret? How did they overcome life's twists and turns to achieve greatness?

The answer lies in a powerful force that resides within each of us: **passion**.

Passion has been the driving force behind countless achievements and breakthroughs over the ages. When passion meets purpose, amazing things happen. It is the unwavering dedication that pushes artists to create masterpieces, scientists to make groundbreaking discoveries, and entrepreneurs to build thriving businesses.

But what exactly is passion? There is more to it than mere enthusiasm or temporary interest. Passion is a deep-rooted connection to something that is in tune with your very essence. It is a force that compels you to pursue your dreams with courage and determination, regardless of adversity.

Passion

Passion is a strong inclination towards an activity people enjoy or even love. It is something they consider significant and willingly invest their time and energy into (Vallerand et al., 2007, p. 507).

Just like a compass always points north, your true passions are your guiding force, ensuring you stay true to yourself no matter how lost you may feel. When life gets complicated and distractions are everywhere, your passions become your immovable reference point. They remind you of what truly matters to you and guide you toward your authentic self.

In the following pages, we will explore the power of passion and how it can transform your life. Self-awareness is the key that can help you reach your full potential. Through reflective exercises and self-assessment, you will embark on a journey of self-discovery, uncovering your interests, strengths, and purpose.

By understanding your passions, you are able to align your goals with what truly drives you, channeling your energy and focus toward endeavors that bring you fulfillment and purpose.

Is Passion really that important?

By identifying your true passions, you will find a force inside you that goes beyond ambition; it is the source of your long-term motivation and meaningful growth. When you're passionate about something, whether it's a hobby, a cause, or a career, it's like tapping into an endless reservoir of positive energy. You can't get enough of it, and it feels like you were made to do it.

Positive psychology sheds light on passion's vital role in our lives. Research has found that passion leads to increased experiences of positive emotions, flow, psychological well-being, better physical health, and improved performance in our chosen pursuits (Vallerand, 2010).

Passion becomes a guiding force, aligning our goals with our authentic selves and helping us maintain a sense of purpose and fulfillment, even amidst life's complexities and distractions. Having a keen understanding of your passions, you can steer your life in line with your values, contributing to a more fulfilling and contented existence (Vallerand et al., 2003). The power of passion lies in its ability to inspire and energize you, making it a central component in pursuing a life worth living.

Simply put, the remarkable accomplishments of countless individuals throughout history serve as a testament to one undeniable truth: passion is the key to success. So now the first step is to ask yourself: What are my true passions?

Discovering your true passions

Discovering your passions is about exploring what you love, what you're good at, and what truly matters to you. As you embark on this journey, you'll learn a lot about yourself and find things you never knew you had inside you.

Uncovering your passions, talents, and core values will unlock a whole new level of self-awareness and self-empowerment. It's like finding the missing pieces of a puzzle that perfectly fit together, creating a vibrant and authentic picture of yourself.

In this quest, you'll find that your passions are not simply hobbies or fleeting interests. They are the key to achieving your full potential and unleashing your creativity. You can rely on them to propel you to overcome any obstacle. When you align your goals with what truly drives you, you set yourself on a natural, authentic, and fulfilling path.

Best-selling author Ken Robinson says, "Finding your passion changes everything. People in their Element connect with something fundamental to their identity, purpose, and well-being." Finding our element involves knowing ourselves, looking at our lives, and observing what we are passionate about and what we have a unique capacity for.

There's no one-size-fits-all approach when it comes to uncovering your true passions. Each person's journey is unique, but I'd love to share the formula that has been an absolute game-changer for me. It's a simple yet powerful combination of three key ingredients - Interests, Strengths, and Values.

My Secret Formula:
Interests - Strengths - Values

First, you start by exploring a wide range of activities and hobbies that genuinely spark your curiosity and bring joy to your life. Next, you identify your natural strengths and talents, as your passions often emerge from what you excel at. Lastly, tune into your core values and align your pursuits with what truly matters to you. When your passions harmonize with your values, you'll experience a profound sense of purpose and fulfillment, creating an authentic and deeply satisfying life.

Now, the magic happens as you combine these three elements to create the ultimate formula for discovering your passions. Embrace your Interests, dive deep into your Strengths, and tune into your Values. Look for the intersection where your interests align with your strengths and both are in tune with your core values. It's at this magical point where your true passions lie!

Remember, discovering your passion is a unique and personal journey. It may take time, experimentation, and self-reflection. Embrace the process with patience and curiosity, and allow yourself to grow and evolve along the way. It is not about perfection or comparison. It's about embracing your individuality, what makes you uniquely you. As the renowned author Elizabeth Gilbert once said, "You are allowed to be both a masterpiece and a work in progress simultaneously." So, enjoy exploring, celebrate your strengths, and stay true to your values. Let's get to work!

Explore your interests

It's no surprise that to discover your passions, the first step is to wonder about what you truly love doing. And guess what? This isn't just my opinion; research has my back.

A study by Kruger and Dunning (1999) sheds light on the importance of exploring interests for personal growth. Their research revealed that people often underestimate their abilities in areas they are genuinely skilled at, leading to missed opportunities to embrace their passions and talents.

This means that by actively engaging in diverse activities and experiences, you can overcome self-doubt and better understand what truly clicks with you.

The activity below aims to help you explore various interests and hobbies and gain insights into how these activities reflect different aspects of your personality and character. By trying out various activities, you can uncover new facets of yourself and identify potential passions.

By the end of this activity, you'll be closer to unveiling your true interests and discovering the passions that bring meaning to your life.

Below is a list of various interests and hobbies. Select six activities that intrigue you or capture your curiosity, bearing in mind that this list is not exhaustive. These activities should cover a broad spectrum to allow you to explore diverse facets of your personality.

- Traveling
- Reading
- Blogging and Podcasting
- Social Media
- Visual Arts
- Writing
- Cooking and Fooding
- Dancing
- Volunteering
- Sports
- Playing a Musical Instrument
- Music Production
- Yoga
- Language Proficiency
- Gardening
- Crafts and DIY
- Weightlifting
- Event Organization
- Interior Design and Decoration
- Outdoor Activities
- Makeup Artistry
- Online Learning
- Computer Repairs
- Martial Arts
- Calligraphy and Lettering
- Recycling

- Collecting
- Camping
- Running
- Chess
- Repairing Objects
- Investing in Real Estate
- Debating
- Photography

Reflect on Your Discoveries: After selecting each activity, take time to reflect on the reasons behind that decision. Consider the emotions, thoughts, and insights that emerge when you think about it. Ask yourself: What do you enjoy about the activity? Does it match any particular aspect of your personality or interests? How does it make you feel?

Identify Common Themes: As you reflect on the different activities, notice any emerging patterns or common themes. Are there activities that align with certain aspects of your personality or values? Are there interests that evoke a strong sense of joy and fulfillment?

You may begin to uncover your passions based on your reflections and the patterns you identified. Pay attention to the activities that resonate deeply with your core being, as these likely reveal significant aspects of yourself.

Extra!

Try Each Activity: Over the next few weeks or months. Embrace each experience with an open mind and heart. Pay attention to how you feel during and after each activity.

As experts in positive psychology affirm, passion is a powerful force that can lead to a life of happiness and well-being. And it all begins with discovering your interests. According to psychologist Mihaly Csikszentmihalyi (1996), when you engage in activities that challenge your skills and provide a sense of fulfillment, you enter a state of flow, complete immersion, and focus. This state enhances your performance and brings joy and a sense of accomplishment.

The activity above invites you to explore various hobbies and activities, each offering a unique perspective into your character and preferences. By trying out these activities and reflecting on your experiences, you can uncover hidden passions and gain valuable insights into who you are.

Focus on your strengths

Some years ago, shortly after starting my career in the IT industry, I had a stable job but began to feel a lingering dissatisfaction. Being someone who's always been curious and eager to learn and grow, I knew it was time to embark on a journey of self-improvement. During this transformative period, I stumbled upon the fascinating world of Character Strengths theory, and little did I know that this discovery would forever change my outlook on life.

As I delved deeper into this theory (I'll explain more about it shortly), I quickly discovered that I had a natural talent for problem-solving and a genuine knack for connecting with people. Quite unexpectedly, my natural talents aligned with the skills needed to succeed as an entrepreneur. Inspired by this realization, I decided to take a leap of faith and venture into the world of entrepreneurship. So, I started a non-profit computer training program and launched a technical staffing and small business consulting company.

As I built my business around my strengths, I felt empowered and fulfilled like never before. Leveraging my problem-solving skills, I could easily navigate complex situations, and my ability to connect with people allowed me to build strong relationships with my students, clients, and employees.

The more I focused on my strengths and passions, the more motivated and engaged I became. With each success, my self-confidence grew, and I realized that I had tapped into my full potential. Embracing my strengths elevated my business and transformed my overall outlook on life.

Looking back, I now realize that understanding myself was directly correlated with my decision to pursue a new path. It wasn't merely a leap into the unknown but a leap grounded in a deeper understanding of myself and my potential for success. Learning about my natural strengths gave me the validation to take that brave step forward.

Focusing on my abilities has transformed my career and enriched my personal life. It has allowed me to cultivate resilience in the face of challenges and maintain a positive mindset.

• The Character Strengths Theory

Have you ever paused to reflect on what makes you strong and virtuous? It's a profound and timeless question that has fascinated cultures and civilizations across the globe for centuries.

Over the years, researchers like the distinguished Martin Seligman and his colleagues have tirelessly studied human behavior and identified six core virtues that seem to be in common with people from diverse backgrounds and cultures. These virtues are courage, humanity, justice, wisdom, temperance, and transcendence. You might wonder, "What do these virtues even mean, and how do they relate to my everyday life?"

Essentially, these virtues serve as the foundation for positive character traits that shape who you are and how you navigate the world. They are like the building blocks of a meaningful and fulfilling life. Each of these virtues gives rise to specific character strengths, those unique qualities that make you who you are and empower you to create a life that truly matters.

Let's take a closer look at each of these virtues and their character strengths:

THE 24 CHARACTERS OF STRENGTH

Reflecting on your strengths is an essential step in understanding yourself better and reaching your full potential. Martin Seligman's theory of character strengths provides a framework to help you identify and embrace your unique virtues.

Using your past experiences as a guide, with the next activity, you will be able to recognize your strengths and use them to enhance your life and well-being. Remember! No right or wrong answers exist, so respond honestly based on your thoughts, feelings, and behaviors.

In this activity, we'll revisit moments from your life where you faced various challenges and triumphs. By reflecting on these experiences, you'll uncover the character strengths that helped you navigate them. Put pen to paper, and let's get started!

Take a moment to reflect on different periods of your life, from adolescence to adulthood. Recall specific situations that left a lasting impression on you, whether challenging or rewarding. These situations can include personal achievements, times of difficulty, or memorable interactions with others.

Select three of the most impactful situations you recalled: one that was challenging, one that was rewarding, and one that involved connecting with others. Take a few minutes to write down brief descriptions of each situation.

Next, analyze each situation and identify the character strengths you utilized to navigate through them. Consider the following questions for each scenario:

a. Challenging Situation: What obstacles did you face, and how did you overcome them? Did you display perseverance, bravery, or creativity to find a solution?

b. Rewarding Situation: What made this moment fulfilling for you? Did you use your love of learning, kindness, or leadership skills to achieve success?

c. Connecting with Others: How did you establish meaningful connections with others? Were your social intelligence, empathy, or teamwork abilities in action?

Take a moment to reflect on your identified strengths in each situation. Acknowledge how these strengths contributed to your personal growth and well-being. Express gratitude for having these qualities, as they have helped shape the person you are today.

Now that you have a deeper understanding of your character strengths challenge yourself to use them intentionally in your current life. Seek opportunities to apply these strengths in everyday situations, relationships, and activities. Embrace your strengths, and let them guide you towards greater confidence and personal growth.

Extra!

If you want to know more about your strengths and dive deeper into the fascinating world of character virtues, check out the VIA Survey! Based on Martin Seligman's research and positive psychology, this scientifically validated tool will help you uncover your unique character strengths and gain valuable insights into what makes you shine.

You can access the VIA Survey online, and it typically takes about 15-20 minutes to complete.

The activity above allows you to travel back in time and rediscover the character strengths that have shaped your journey. By reflecting on past experiences, both challenging and rewarding, you'll gain a deeper appreciation for the unique qualities that make you strong and virtuous.

Amazingly, you can return to this exercise as often as needed. I've found myself returning to it whenever I need a boost of confidence and self-awareness. Each time I do, I discover new layers of strength within myself, filling me with a sense of empowerment.

Tune into your values

You're probably familiar with the movie "The Social Network." If not, it is about how a young entrepreneur, Mark Zuckerberg, created Facebook. He's portrayed as a passionate and socially awkward student at Harvard University, and to your surprise, he's an excellent example of someone whose passions align with their values.

Simply put, values are the things that matter most to us, the guiding principles that shape who we are and what we believe in. For Mark, his values included the idea that connecting people is essential, everyone deserves a voice, and challenging the norms of how people interact is exciting.

On the other hand, passion is burning enthusiasm for something we truly love or care about (you probably already know this at this point). For Mark, his passion was computer programming and creating innovative technologies.

Here's where the magic happens: When Mark's passion for computer programming and his values of connecting people come together, he gets inspired to build something incredible that changes our reality forever: Facebook. His desire to challenge how people interact and create a platform for connecting them fuels his entrepreneurial journey.

Throughout the movie, we can see how his passion for technology and connecting people drives him to overcome challenges and keep working towards his goal, even when things get tough. His belief in connecting people and giving them a voice motivates him to succeed.

Mark's story shows us the power of aligning our passions with our values. Doing something we love that aligns with what we deeply care about gives us a sense of purpose and fulfillment. It becomes easier to stay committed, even when faced with obstacles

A study by Vallerand and Houlfort (2003) found that when passion was aligned with one's values and personal identity, it was positively associated with well-being, life satisfaction, and positive emotions.

So, if you're looking to build something meaningful in your life, start by identifying what truly matters to you and find that sweet spot where your passions and values meet. In the next exercise, we will delve into the meaning of values and their profound impact on our lives. By identifying and prioritizing your values, you can gain clarity on what truly holds meaning in your life and guide your decisions and actions accordingly. That's where your journey to success and fulfillment begins!

Passion, though powerful, needs direction, and that is where our values come into play. So, let's pause for a moment and reflect.

To begin, let's revisit the meaning of values: they are the pillars of integrity, standing resolute amidst the winds of life's boundless circumstances. They are how you want to behave as a human being. They are not about what you want to achieve but rather about how you want to treat yourself, others, and the world around you.

By identifying and prioritizing your values, you can gain clarity on what truly matters to you, allowing you to make decisions and take actions that align with your deepest desires.

Since I know you might not be an expert in values (I certainly am not), I have compiled a list of common values you can use. This list was proposed by Russ Harris (2022), a prominent expert in Acceptance and Commitment Therapy (ACT) and the author of numerous books on mindfulness and psychological well-being. Take your time to read through the list below and carefully contemplate each value.

The challenge for you is to pick seven values that deeply speak to you. Afterward, arrange them in order of priority, reflecting the values that hold the most significance for you at whatever stage in your life you're in. This exercise aims to provide you with a clearer understanding of what truly defines you and what matters most in your journey.

Ambition	Authenticity	Beauty	Change
Compassion	Confidence	Cooperation	Courage
Creativity	Diversity	Enjoyment	Fairness
Freedom	Friendship	Frugality	Generosity
Health and Wellness	Honesty	Influence	Justice
Kindness	Knowledge	Love	Loyalty
Nature	Order	Peace	Personal Development
Popularity	Recognition	Reputation	Security
Simplicity	Strength	Teamwork	Timeliness
Tolerance	Understanding	Uniqueness	Curiosity

Take some time to reflect on how living by these top seven values aligns with your passions, desires, and aspirations. Consider how embracing these values can lead to a more fulfilling and purpose-driven life.

1.

2.

3.

4.

5.

6.

7.

As we conclude this first chapter on building a life worth living, we find ourselves at the core of self-awareness, the powerful force that can bring out the true potential of our passions. As research suggests, passion alone is not enough; it requires mindfulness and reflection to become the transformative force it can be.

Our journey begins with understanding this fundamental truth: to control your destiny, you must first identify your true passions.

By being mindful of your passions, you can better understand your intrinsic drivers and align your goals with what truly motivates you.

The formula I've shared with you—exploring your interests, focusing on your strengths, and tuning into your values—provides a practical approach to identifying and aligning your passions with your goals.

In the end, discovering your passions is not just a whimsical pursuit; it's a journey that can bring about positive changes in every aspect of your life. By exploring your interests, embracing your strengths, and aligning with your core values, you unlock the door to a more authentic and fulfilling existence.

With this newfound self-awareness, you are now equipped to step into Chapter 2, which is focused on the next crucial step: setting SMART goals. Now that your true passions guide you, setting specific, measurable, achievable, relevant, and time-bound goals will help you reach your objectives.

Chapter 1

Key takeaways

- Passion is a powerful force that, when aligned with your purpose, can lead to extraordinary achievements and fulfillment in life.
- Passion is an intense devotion to an activity you enjoy and consider significant. It involves a deep-rooted connection to something that resonates with your essence.
- Your true passions act as a compass, guiding you through life's complexities and distractions, reminding you of what truly matters.
- Identifying your true passions is essential because they provide long-term motivation, meaningful growth, and positive energy in pursuing your goals.
- Research in positive psychology shows that passion leads to increased positive emotions, psychological well-being, better physical health, and improved performance in chosen pursuits.
- Discovering your passions involves a combination of interests, strengths, and values. When these three elements align, you find your true passions.
- Reflecting on various interests and hobbies helps uncover your passions. Experimenting with different activities can reveal new facets of yourself.
- Understanding your character strengths and using them intentionally can lead to personal growth, confidence, and a sense of purpose.

- Martin Seligman's theory of character strengths identifies virtues that give rise to specific character traits. Recognizing your strengths can empower you to create a more fulfilling life.
- Aligning your passions with your values can lead to a sense of purpose and motivation. Your values guide your actions and decisions.
- Identifying and prioritizing your values helps clarify what matters most to you and allows you to make decisions in line with your deepest desires.
- Self-awareness is crucial for understanding your passions. It requires reflection, exploring interests, and recognizing strengths and values.
- Exploring interests, focusing on strengths, and tuning into values provide a practical approach to identifying and aligning your passions with your goals.
- Discovering your passions is not a whimsical pursuit but a journey that positively impacts all aspects of your life, leading to authenticity and fulfillment.

SET MEANINGFUL GOALS

"You are never too old to set another goal or to dream a new dream."

- *C.S. Lewis*

W e have all seen the classic underdog story, "Rocky." Imagine you are Rocky Balboa, a man with raw talent and a burning desire to become a champion. In Chapter 1, you discover your true passion, the boxing ring, where you can feel the fire in your belly.

But passion alone doesn't guarantee victory. As the story unfolds, Rocky realizes that to stand a chance against the reigning champion, he needs more than just heart. Something similar happens in real life. Goals without plans are nothing more than wishes. Hence, **setting smart objectives is crucial for moving from dreaming big to taking action.**

Like Rocky's trainer, Mickey guided him through the grueling preparation; Chapter 2 will introduce your own Mickey: the SMART goals framework. It will be your cornerman whispering valuable advice in your ear, leading you to a fulfilling life.

If you are unfamiliar with them, SMART goals are a robust framework for setting goals proposed by George T. Doran in 1981, empowering you to set meaningful aspirations. These goals are not just dreams floating in the distance but tangible targets inspiring action and providing a roadmap for progress.

You know that stepping into the ring with Apollo Creed unprepared would be a disaster. In the same way, SMART goals keep you grounded and ensure your objectives are Specific, Measurable, Achievable, Relevant, and Time-bound. They challenge you, but they're always within reach. They push you further like Rocky running up those iconic stairs.

Just as Rocky transformed from an underdog to a hero, you too can start on your journey to success with SMART goals by your side. This chapter is your training ground, where you'll discover the art of setting meaningful objectives and pushing beyond your limits.

Extra!

Before diving into the chapter, take a moment to jot down your goals list. Don't worry about making it perfect right now; the key is to get your thoughts down on paper. As you progress through the content in this chapter, you'll gain valuable insights on how to transform your goals into SMART goals.

Understanding the importance of setting meaningful and aligned goals

Goal setting is common practice, particularly when we begin our "New Year's Resolutions" journey each year. However, we lose track of or abandon these goals as time passes. Have you ever wondered why this happens?

Perhaps the reason lies in the misalignment between our aspirations and true desires for the future. Here's why setting meaningful and aligned goals is crucial to success.

What is a meaningful goal, and why is it important?

Meaningful goals

Goals driven by internal motivation add exponential value over time by making you more efficient and effective at what you do while guiding you toward greater self-authenticity

Choosing basic and uninteresting goals may seem easy initially, but as you work towards them, you may need more drive to persist through challenges and obstacles.

However, here's the crucial point: Motivation comes from setting meaningful goals. Staying the course becomes much easier when you choose goals that mean something in your life. **This is because**

achieving those goals will positively impact your overall well-being and happiness in the long run.

There is no doubt that this is easier said than done. Ensuring that your goals and objectives align with your values and purpose is challenging. To do so, you must find those aspirations that resonate with who you are and make you say, " Yes! This is what I want!"

Despite how hard it is, establishing meaningful and aligned objectives that resonate with your core values and long-term aspirations is worth the effort. This will give you clarity, focus, and motivation, propelling you toward personal growth and fulfillment. Goals should not be set for the sake of tradition. Instead, make sure to explore your inner self, dig into your true passions, and set goals that align with the grand vision you have for your life.

Setting meaningful goals will change your life in 3 ways		
Clarity and Focus	**Motivation and Resilience**	**Personal Growth and Fulfillment**
When you set meaningful goals, you gain clarity about what truly matters to you. With a clear goal, you can prioritize your efforts, and distractions become less tempting. This focused approach allows you to channel your time and energy into activities that resonate with your purpose, propelling you closer to your ultimate vision.	Meaningful goals serve as powerful motivators. When your aspirations are deeply rooted in your values and passions, you are more likely to stay committed and persistent, even when faced with challenges. Meaningful goals provide the fuel to keep you going, empowering you to overcome obstacles and bounce back from setbacks with renewed determination.	Aligned goals catalyze personal growth and fulfillment. They push you out of your comfort zone and encourage you to develop new skills and abilities. As you progress, you gain a sense of accomplishment and satisfaction, knowing you live authentically and in harmony with your deepest aspirations.

Extra!

In the first chapter, you discovered your core values. For meaningful goals to be achieved, you must build on these principles.

Before setting your goals, revisit Chapter 1 to refresh your true passions and core values.

Your life will be better if you have meaningful goals; science tells us

Recognizing the connection between goal-setting and overall life satisfaction is not just a subjective belief; it is supported by scientific research. Numerous studies have shown that goal-setting improves well-being and life satisfaction. Here are some reasons that support the relevance of this connection:

- **Sense of Purpose and Direction:** Experts affirm that setting meaningful and achievable goals provides individuals with a sense of purpose and direction in life. When people have clear objectives, they are more likely to feel motivated and focused, knowing their efforts have a specific purpose. This sense of purpose contributes to a greater sense of fulfillment and life satisfaction.

- **Enhanced Psychological Well-Being:** Goal-setting has been linked to improved psychological well-being. Studies show that when individuals set and achieve their goals, they experience a sense of accomplishment and self-efficacy. This positive feedback loop boosts self-esteem, confidence, and overall emotional well-being, leading to greater life satisfaction.

- **Reduction in Stress and Anxiety:** Goals provide structure and organization in one's life. When individuals have clear objectives and a plan to achieve them, they tend to experience reduced stress and anxiety levels. This is because goal-setting can help individuals break down complex tasks into manageable steps, making the overall journey less overwhelming and stressful.

- **Sense of Control and Autonomy:** Having well-defined goals gives individuals a sense of control and autonomy over their lives. When people actively participate in setting their objectives and work towards achieving them, they feel empowered and in charge of their destinies. This sense of control contributes significantly to life satisfaction and overall happiness.

Altogether, scientific research consistently demonstrates that goal-setting plays a crucial role in enhancing overall life satisfaction. Setting and pursuing meaningful objectives provides individuals with a sense of purpose, improves psychological well-being, reduces stress, and fosters a sense of control over one's life.

However, it doesn't stop there. The beauty of goal-setting is that it shapes your life in a way that aligns with what truly matters to you. When you're living a life that aligns with your deepest desires, satisfaction becomes your faithful companion.

Strategies for effective goal-setting

How do SMART goals work? It's a simple yet effective framework that ensures your goals hit all the right notes.

SMART stands for Specific - Measurable -Achievable - Relevant - Time-bound.

Specific: Setting goals that are clear and well-defined.

When setting goals, being concrete and straightforward is vital for success. A well-known entrepreneur, Jon Taffer, once said: "Simple things can be really powerful."

Ever set a goal only to forget its details the day after? It may have needed to be simplified or more specific for you to remember. That's why it is so important to be precise. This does not mean settling for mediocrity or avoiding challenges. Simply put, it means setting an easy-to-understand goal that anyone can grasp.

There is no need for lengthy, complicated objectives that overwhelm and discourage you. Instead, focus on simplicity and clarity. Setting goals requires getting to the heart of what you want to achieve. Craft your goals in a way that leaves no room for doubt.

Here are some examples of what setting specific or vague goals would look like.

Specific goals	Vague goals
I will complete a 10K race in under 1 hour by the end of this year.	I want to get healthier.
I will save $5,000 over the next 12 months for a down payment on a house.	Learn how to save money.
I will complete three online courses in web development	I want to learn new skills.
I will lose 15 pounds in the next three months	Lose weight.

Many times, being vague is often a typical characteristic when setting goals. While being vague is easier, it is inefficient in the long run. So it is the first mistake that should be avoided.

Extra!

Go back to your goals list and ask yourself, are they specific? How clear and detailed are your goals? Do they answer the 5 W's; who, what, where, when, and why? For instance, if your goal is to "get healthier," try refining it to "exercise for 25 minutes, six days a week, to improve cardiovascular health and increase overall fitness."

Measurable: *Establishing quantifiable criteria to track progress.*

One of the pillars of SMART goals is "Measurable," which involves establishing quantifiable criteria to track your progress. Measurable goals can be tracked with simple reference points. As a general rule, you want to be able to quantify your success, whether in terms of size, amount, duration, or mass.

When your goals are measurable, you gain a clear understanding of your achievements and can make informed adjustments along the way. Think of it as having a GPS guiding you towards success, allowing you to celebrate each milestone you hit.

A 3-Step Guide to crafting measurable goals

As the saying goes, "What gets measured gets managed." Here is how to set measurable goals that serve as your compass toward triumph.

Step 1

Define Clear Objectives

The first step to creating measurable goals is to define clear and specific objectives. Take a moment to contemplate what you truly want to achieve. Your objectives should be crystal-clear, leaving no room for ambiguity. Ask yourself the following questions:

- What do I want to accomplish?
- How will I measure my progress toward this goal?
- What specific results do I want to see?

For example, if your goal is to improve your physical fitness, a clear objective could be "I want to run a 5K race within the next three months."

Step 2

Quantify Your Success

Now that you have defined your objectives, it's time to quantify your success. Measurable goals require concrete criteria that allow you to track your progress. Consider the following ways to quantify your success:

- **Numeric Values:** Set specific numbers to measure your progress. It could be the number of pounds lost, the amount of money saved, or the percentage of tasks completed.
- **Timeframes:** Establish deadlines or timeframes to achieve your goals. Having a specific end date adds urgency and focus to your efforts.

Using the fitness example, you could quantify your success by setting a target time to complete the 5K race, such as "I want to complete the 5K race in under 30 minutes."

Step 3

3

Track Your Progress and Celebrate Milestones

The final step is to track your progress and celebrate milestones. Regularly monitor your journey towards measurable goals using tools like journals, apps, or charts. Keep a record of your achievements and setbacks to assess your advancement accurately.

Breaking your long-term goal into smaller milestones makes the journey more manageable. Celebrate each milestone you achieve, as these minor victories fuel your motivation and build your confidence to reach the ultimate objective.

In the fitness example, you can track your weekly running distance, pace, and time. Celebrate reaching milestones like running your first mile without stopping, running your first 5K training session, and achieving new personal bests.

Extra!

Now, let's go back to your goals list and ask yourself, are they measurable? Take a moment to evaluate how well you can quantify your progress toward each goal. Do your goals have concrete reference points that allow you to track your achievements?

To ensure your goals are measurable, consider the following questions:

- Can you set specific numeric values to measure your progress?
- Have you established clear timeframes or deadlines to achieve your goals?
- Can you track your advancements with tangible metrics?

Take the time to make your goals measurable, and let them guide you toward a successful life.

Achievable: *Setting realistic and attainable goals.*

One of the keys to success is ensuring that your goals are reachable. Finding the sweet spot between ambition and realism lays the foundation for progress. It keeps you motivated on your journey toward greatness. But you might wonder, how do you set realistic goals while still nurturing your ambitious spirit? Here's the answer.

Balancing Ambition with Reality

While setting challenging goals is essential for growth, it's vital to ensure that they are within the realm of possibility, not only within your capabilities but if your surroundings can let you reach it.

Pushing yourself to reach new heights with stretch goals is fantastic, but setting unattainable goals can lead to frustration and demotivation. Consider factors such as available resources, time constraints, and current circumstances. Aim for goals that require effort and stretch your limits while being realistic and attainable.

A great example of the delicate art of balancing ambition with reality is the movie "The Pursuit of Happiness." Based on a true story, the protagonist, Chris Gardner (played by Will Smith), is a struggling salesman and single father facing financial hardships and homelessness. Despite his challenging circumstances, he aspires to become a successful stockbroker, a seemingly unattainable goal given his lack of formal education and financial resources.

Chris' ambition to achieve his dream is admirable, and he pushes himself to the limit by taking on a position at a prestigious brokerage firm as an unpaid intern. However, he also grapples with the reality of his situation, constantly balancing his responsibilities as a father and the limited time and resources at his disposal.

Chris encounters numerous obstacles and setbacks throughout the film, testing his resilience and determination. Despite facing overwhelming odds, he never lets go of his dream. Still, he continually reassesses his approach to make it more feasible and attainable.

The turning point comes when Chris realizes that he must balance his ambitious aspirations and the pragmatic reality he faces. He doesn't give up on his goal. Instead, he refines his strategy, focusing on providing for his son's well-being while diligently pursuing his internship.

As the movie portrays, setting achievable goals is about finding the balance between pushing yourself and staying grounded. **Assess your capabilities, leverage your resources, and strike a balance that allows you to stretch your limits without overwhelming yourself.**

By setting realistic and attainable goals, you set yourself up for success, boost your confidence, and maintain the motivation to crush those goals like a pro.

Identifying your strengths and resources

Our environment is beyond our control, but thankfully we can always focus on improving ourselves. There will be some things you cannot control regarding how achievable your goals are, but there will also be other things you can control.

For this reason, let's take a moment to assess your capabilities and resources. Throughout Chapter 1, we discussed your character strengths and now is definitely a good time to refresh them. Are you a skilled communicator, a problem solver, or a creative thinker? Allow your self-awareness to guide you toward setting goals that perfectly match your abilities. Consider your unique set of skills, knowledge, and experiences. Having self-awareness will maximize your chances of success.

By recognizing your strengths and limitations, you can set realistic expectations and design a plan that utilizes your strengths while addressing potential challenges.

Step 1: Reflect on Your Character Strengths

Take a moment to reflect on the character strengths we discussed in Chapter 1. These strengths include qualities like creativity, perseverance, kindness, leadership, and more. Write down a list of character strengths that resonate with you the most. Be honest with yourself and acknowledge the strengths that you genuinely possess.

Step 2: Identify Your Skills and Experiences

Now, shift your focus to your skills and experiences. Think about the activities, tasks, or projects you have excelled in the past. What are the things that come naturally to you? What skills have you honed over time? Jot down these skills and experiences in your journal.

Step 3: Embrace Your Self-Awareness

With your list of character strengths, skills, and experiences, take a moment to embrace your self-awareness. Recognize and appreciate the unique combination of strengths you possess. Allow yourself to feel confident in your capabilities, knowing that these strengths are your assets for achieving success.

Step 4: Address Potential Challenges

As you set your goals, also consider potential challenges that may arise. How can you use your strengths to overcome these challenges? Think about strategies and resources that can support you in tackling obstacles along the way.

Extra!

Rethink your goals to make them more realistic. Now that you understand your strengths and resources more clearly, it's time to align them with your goals. Go back to your initial list and start thinking of ways to leverage your strengths to achieve these goals.

Remember, this activity is not just a one-time exercise. Revisit your strengths regularly and update your goals as you continue to grow and develop. Embrace your unique qualities and embark on a journey of self-improvement. **You have the power to create your own path when you know what your strengths are and are determined to achieve what you desire.**

Relevant: Ensuring goals align with personal values and aspirations

The SMART goals theory reminds us that relevance is a crucial element in our goal-setting journey. When your goals align with your values, passions, and aspirations, they become powerful, propelling you toward meaningful success.

The term implies that something is suitable for a particular purpose. In other words, if you are setting a goal, it should be meaningful to you!

For example, let's consider two scenarios:

- **Scenario 1:** You wish to learn a new musical instrument but don't have a passion for music. This goal might not be relevant to your interests or hold little meaning in your life.
- **Scenario 2:** Your goal is to start a real estate brokerage based on your love for helping those who have dreams of home ownership. This goal aligns with your passion and values, making it more relevant and significant to your life's purpose.

Relevant goals have a profound impact on our motivation and commitment. Our intrinsic motivation soars when we pursue objectives that genuinely matter to us. Studies have shown that individuals who set relevant goals are more likely to persist in their efforts and stay committed to achieving them (Locke & Latham, 2006).

Exploring the Connection between Goal Alignment and Intrinsic Motivation

As we have said before, aligning your goals with your values and aspirations taps into the power of intrinsic motivation.

When your goals are connected to these core values and desires, you'll find a deep sense of purpose and passion that fuels your motivation. By understanding the intrinsic motivations behind your goals, you can ensure that they resonate with who you are and what you want to achieve.

In my own journey, this connection between goal alignment and intrinsic motivation played a crucial role in bringing this book to life. I turned my core values and passion for empowering others into SMART goals. Embracing my desire to make a positive impact on people's lives, I knew I needed a clear and structured approach to achieve this dream.

With a passionate drive to help others, I set out to write a guide that would deeply resonate with my readers and inspire them to forge their destinies. I knew I could create a book that would positively impact people's lives if I stayed true to my purpose and aligned my objectives with the message I wanted to share.

In summary, never underestimate the power of intrinsic motivation. When your goals align with your values and what you truly desire, it ignites an intense passion that drives you toward success. Embracing this link between goal alignment and intrinsic motivation enables you to lead a fulfilling life with purpose and meaning for yourself and those around you. As you nurture this connection, you create a journey filled with authenticity, inspiration, and meaningful achievements.

Extra!

Go back to your goals list and ask yourself, are they Relevant? Take some time to assess the relevance of each goal. Focus your efforts on those closely aligning with your long-term goals and core values. If a goal does not contribute to your overall vision, consider whether it's worth pursuing or if it's better to redirect your energy toward more meaningful objectives.

To ensure your goals are relevant, consider the following questions:

- How does this daily goal contribute to my long-term vision?
- Does achieving this objective bring me closer to embodying my core values?
- Is this goal relevant to the person I want to become and the life I want to lead?

Time-bound: Assigning deadlines and creating a sense of urgency

Time-bound goals are restricted in time, which is crucial when setting goals. Keeping yourself accountable and driving progress requires clear deadlines.

Why do I need a timeline?

When you assign specific deadlines to your goals, you give them a sense of urgency and accountability. In other words, a certain level of pressure and motivation kicks in when you have a deadline to meet. It's like having a clock ticking in the background, reminding you to stay focused and get things done.

With a deadline, goals can quickly become clear and concrete. They might stay in your mind, waiting for the perfect moment to pursue it. But as we all know, the ideal moment rarely comes. Setting a clear timeframe transforms those goals from distant dreams into tangible targets.

Having a deadline brings a level of commitment and focus to your goals. It's like making a promise to yourself that you'll make it happen within a specific timeframe. It creates a sense of responsibility towards your objectives, and you're more likely to act proactively towards them.

Be realistic

When setting time frames for your goals, you must be mindful of your available time. Take a moment to consider your daily schedule and how you'll allocate time for each task.

Think of it as sketching out your day, planning when you'll work on your goal, and setting realistic deadlines to ensure you can accomplish it. Avoid falling into the trap of overloading your day with tasks, as it can lead to stress and unmet expectations.

We've all been there: studying for a final exam and realizing we didn't finish any of the tasks in time and with the quality we wanted. Trust me; you don't want that to happen with your life goals. That's why being honest about your time limitations is crucial. It's the first step to setting yourself up for success.

By setting realistic deadlines, you give yourself the space to work diligently and stay on track without feeling overwhelmed. Remember, it's okay to take baby steps and make steady progress. Rushing towards a goal may lead to burnout and diminish the quality of your efforts.

Here are some aspects you can consider to be sure your Goals are time-bound.

- **Define Specific Deadlines:** Review each goal on your list and determine a specific deadline for achieving it. Ask yourself:
  - When do I want to accomplish this goal?
  - Can I set a specific date or time frame for its completion?
- **Break Down Long-Term Goals:** For longer-term or more complex goals, consider breaking them down into smaller milestones with

clear deadlines. This will help keep you inspired and allow you to track your progress more effectively. Ask yourself:

- What intermediate milestones can I set to reach this long-term goal?
- What is a realistic timeframe for achieving each milestone?

- **Use Time-Based Metrics:** To make your goals time-bound, incorporate time-based metrics that allow you to track your advancements. For example, you can measure progress in hours, days, weeks, or months, depending on the nature of the goal. Ask yourself:

  - How can I track my progress over time?
  - What time-based metrics can I use to monitor my achievements?

- **Set Reminders and Review Points:** Establish regular review points on your calendar to assess your progress and make any necessary adjustments to your goals. Setting reminders will help you stay accountable and ensure that you are on the right track. Ask yourself:

  - How often should I review my progress toward each goal?
  - How can I stay on top of my deadlines and ensure I'm making steady progress?

Extra!

Take a look at your goals list and assess whether they are time-bound, meaning, do you have clear timeframes or deadlines set for each goal? Time-bound goals help keep you focused, accountable, and on track to achieve your desired outcomes. Let's ensure your goals are time-bound by considering the questions above.

Making your goals time-bound gives you a sense of urgency and purpose. This focus on deadlines empowers you to manage your time efficiently and make the most of every moment on your journey. Let the time-bound aspect of SMART goals get you closer to success.

Putting it all together

Setting *SMART* goals

Main goal:

Start by clearly defining your main goal. Be specific about what you want to achieve, ensuring your goal is clear and concise.

_____

_____

_____

Is it measurable?

Consider whether you can track your progress with specific metrics or measurements. Can you quantify your success and set milestones to monitor your advancement?

_____

_____

_____

Is it achievable?

Assess whether your goal is realistic and attainable. Take into account your capabilities, resources, and any potential challenges you might face.

_____

_____

_____

Does it resonate with you?

Reflect on whether this goal aligns with your core values and aspirations. Ensure that it is meaningful and important to you, as this will fuel your motivation.

_____

_____

_____

Now that it is ready, set a time frame.

Establish a clear time frame or deadline for achieving your goal. Set specific dates to create a sense of urgency and keep yourself accountable.

_____

_____

_____

Tracking progress

Let's discuss one final important aspect: keeping your goals in mind. It happens yearly. You make your New Year's resolutions and forget about them, right? Don't let it slide anymore. Stay on track, and don't lose sight of your goals! Here are three key ways to keep yourself in touch with your goals.

- **Making reminders**

  Harness the power of technology and use calendar or phone reminders to keep your goals at the forefront of your mind. Set regular reminders to check your progress, review your goals, and take necessary actions.

  Whether it's a daily, weekly, or monthly reminder, notifications will prompt you to stay engaged and ensure you don't forget about your goals amidst the hustle and bustle of daily life.

- **Use a habit tracker**

  Incorporating a habit tracker into your routine can be a game-changer. Whether it's a physical journal, a habit-tracking app, or a simple checklist, these tools help you visually track your progress and hold yourself accountable.

- **Set a time of your week to keep in touch with your goals**

  Make your goals a priority by scheduling dedicated time each week to focus on them. Set aside a specific day or a few hours each week to review your progress, evaluate your actions, and make any necessary adjustments. This time must be treated as sacred, unchangeable, and non-negotiable, just like any other important commitment in your schedule. Use it to reflect, plan, and strategize how you'll continue working towards your goals.

So, there you have it! Setting goals can be a total game-changer, but making them SMART is what takes you to the next level of growth. We've covered everything about goal-setting: the right way to set them, what qualities to look for, and how to stick with them.

Remember, **consistency is the magic word here.** Don't let your goals slip through your fingers. Keep that fire burning, and stay persistent. The key to success is to stay committed and never give up.

Chapter 2

Key takeaways

- Meaningful goals motivate you intrinsically, improve your effectiveness over time, and help you become more authentic.
- Understanding your core values is essential because not every goal is suitable for everyone. Find that perfect fit that makes you eager to pursue it.
- When you have clear goals in front of you, it's like having a roadmap to your dreams. You know where you're headed, and that sense of direction brings a newfound sense of purpose and fulfillment.
- A specific goal means that it is free from ambiguity, something that is accurate and easy to understand. Learning to simplify your objectives is essential.
- A measurable goal refers to a goal that can be tracked and assessed. You can use metrics and milestones to do so
- An achievable goal is a realistic objective that fits your personal capabilities. It is essential to know yourself to know what to set. Think about your strengths and weaknesses as an exercise.
- When it comes to setting relevant and time-bound goals, it's crucial to establish a strong connection with your intrinsic values. Intrinsic values are those deeply rooted beliefs and principles that define who you are and what truly matters to you. When your goals align with these core values, they become more meaningful and personally significant.

- Additionally, setting time-bound goals means assigning specific deadlines to achieve them. These deadlines act as powerful motivators, urging you to take consistent action and make steady progress.
- It is essential to keep track of your goals and maintain focus. Using reminders, habit trackers, and setting a dedicated time to do so can be an excellent way to make your objectives happen.

CULTIVATE A GROWTH MINDSET

"The only limitations we face in life are those we impose on ourselves"

- James J.

Have you ever wondered how the turtle won the race in the well-known children's story "The Tortoise and the Hare"? Indeed, the odds were stacked against him. The hare was lightning-fast, while the tortoise could barely keep up. Yet, in the end, the tortoise came out victorious, proving that there's more to success than just raw talent.

This children's story teaches us a profound lesson about the power of mindset and how we approach life challenges and opportunities. In this age-old tale, a speedy hare challenges a slow-moving tortoise to a race. The hare underestimates the tortoise's abilities and decides to nap during the race, assuming victory is guaranteed due to its natural speed and talent.

But here's where the story takes an intriguing twist. The tortoise, always thinking of its improvement, is determined to give its best effort despite being slower than the hare. Despite not having the innate speed of a hare, it believes in its ability to keep moving forward and improve through perseverance and hard work.

As the race begins, the hare dashes ahead, leaving the tortoise far behind. Feeling overconfident, the hare decides to rest, assuming it has plenty of time to win the race effortlessly.

Meanwhile, the tortoise continues steadily, never giving up, even though the hare seems almost out of sight. Driven by its growth mindset, the tortoise remains focused on the goal and committed to reaching the finish line.

When the hare wakes, it realizes that the tortoise is approaching the finish line. Panicking, it sprints as fast as it can to catch up, but it's too late. The tortoise crosses the finish line first, achieving victory through determination and persistence.

What about you? As you think about your life journey, do you see yourself more like the hare or the tortoise? Are you someone who relies only on your natural talents without seeking improvement, or are you like the determined tortoise who faces challenges with a positive attitude and keeps trying to do better?

Thinking about this can help you understand how you approach life and deal with success and challenges. It's important to remember that our mindset affects the outcome, just as in the story.

The Mindsets Theory

Carol Dweck, a renowned psychologist, has developed a fascinating theory that can shed light on how we approach life and tackle success and challenges. Think about this theory as a powerful tool for maximizing your potential and better understanding your mindset. The key concept she introduced is called "mindset." At its core, the theory proposes that our beliefs about our intelligence, talents, and abilities fall into two main categories: fixed and growth mindsets. Now, let's break it down in simple terms.

A growth mindset means firmly believing in your ability to improve and achieve remarkable things through hard work and perseverance. It's like knowing you can develop your skills and intelligence over time, like how the tortoise keeps leveling up.

Opposite to this, there's another mindset you can embrace embodied by those who believe their abilities and intelligence are set in stone. The Hare would be an example of this mindset. But let's point something out. The Hare was overconfident about its skills, but that's not always the case. Often, when people face challenges or failures, they may interpret them as signs of their limitations. They might think, "I'm just not smart enough," or "I'll never be good at this." This attitude of believing that your talents and intelligence are fixed and unchangeable is a fixed mindset. Those with a fixed mindset often avoid challenges because they fear failing and believe their inherent abilities define their potential.

Unlike the growth mindset, where effort and perseverance are seen as the path to improvement, a fixed mindset can lead to a sense of helplessness and avoidance of challenges. It limits people's willingness to take risks or step outside their comfort zone because they fear being judged for their perceived shortcomings.

So, rather than thinking that your abilities are fixed and unchangeable, a growth mindset empowers you to embrace challenges and view failures as opportunities to learn and grow. It encourages you to see effort and dedication as the keys to success rather than relying solely on natural talents.

Adopting a growth mindset opens up a world of possibilities and potential. You become more willing to take on challenges, face obstacles confidently, and never shy away from pushing beyond your comfort zone. This approach can lead to more significant achievements, personal growth, and a more fulfilling life.

The good news is that our mindset is not set in stone; it can be changed and cultivated. By becoming aware of our fixed mindset tendencies, we can actively work towards developing a growth mindset. It's all about recognizing that abilities and intelligence can be acquired through dedication and effort.

Fixed Mindset

Growth Mindset

A fixed mindset is the belief that intelligence and abilities are fixed traits that cannot significantly change, leading to avoidance of challenges and a fear of failure (Dweck, 2006).

A growth mindset is a belief that intelligence and abilities can be developed through effort, learning, and perseverance, leading to a willingness to embrace challenges and see failures as opportunities for growth and improvement (Dweck, 2006).

Characteristics of each type

In pursuing personal growth and success, how we perceive our abilities and approach challenges can profoundly affect our results. **This means that growth and fixed mindsets influence our attitudes toward learning, effort, and resilience.** Understanding both mindsets' characteristics can help us better understand our behaviors and beliefs. In this way, we are empowered to make conscious choices about how we live our lives.

The growth mindset, characterized by its belief in the potential for development and improvement, encourages individuals to embrace challenges and view failures as opportunities for learning. It emphasizes the value of effort, hard work, and the understanding that abilities can be cultivated over time. Someone with this mindset admires and learns from the success of others, maintains a positive outlook on personal development, and sees setbacks as temporary hurdles that can be overcome with determination.

On the other hand, the fixed mindset, with its belief in static abilities and talents, may lead individuals to avoid challenges for fear of exposing perceived weaknesses. People with this mindset internalize failures, discouraging the pursuit of learning and growth. They may also feel threatened by others' success, leading to feelings of envy or resentment. Their focus tends to be on achieving immediate success rather than embracing the learning process and appreciating the growth journey.

Growth Mindset	Fixed Mindset
• Welcomes challenges and views them as opportunities to learn and grow.	• Avoids challenges to maintain the illusion of being competent.
• Views failures as stepping stones to improvement and does not take them personally.	• Interprets failures as personal shortcomings and may feel discouraged by them.
• Puts in effort and believes that hard work leads to progress and success.	• Believes that abilities and talents are innate and unchangeable.
• Takes feedback positively and uses it to improve.	• Disregard constructive criticism and may react defensively to feedback.
• Admires and learns from others' success without feeling threatened or envious.	• Feels threatened by others' success and may feel envious or resentful.
• Continuously seeks self-improvement and values the process of learning.	• Avoids situations that might expose perceived weaknesses to others.
• Has a resilient attitude and bounces back from setbacks with determination.	• Views setbacks as evidence of inherent inadequacy and may give up easily.
• Sees obstacles as temporary and surmountable with the right approach.	• Sees obstacles as insurmountable barriers and may feel overwhelmed by them.
• Maintains an optimistic outlook on personal development and life goals.	• Tends to have a negative outlook on personal growth and potential.
• Values the growth journey and does not solely focus on the end result.	• Focuses on achieving immediate success rather than embracing the learning process.

It's essential to remember that people may exhibit characteristics of both mindsets in different situations, and perspectives can be changed and developed with conscious effort and awareness. The goal is to cultivate a growth mindset and embrace the qualities that lead to continuous learning, improvement, and resilience.

By understanding these characteristics, you can identify which mindset predominates in different areas of your life and take proactive steps to develop a growth-oriented approach, unlocking your potential for continuous improvement and personal development.

This activity aims to help you identify which mindset (growth or fixed) you resonate with the most in various aspects of your life. By recognizing your dominant mindset, you can take proactive steps to cultivate a growth-oriented approach and embrace opportunities for personal development.

- When faced with challenging tasks, I feel excited to take them on and push myself to achieve more.
- Learning from failures is a crucial part of my growth journey.
- I consistently put in the time and dedication required to achieve my goals, knowing it will lead to progress and success.

- I tend to avoid challenges and stick with what I know I can do well.
- I worry that if I fail, it will reflect poorly on my abilities and who I am as a person.
- In some areas of my life, I don't put in the effort to develop my abilities and talents because I consider them to be fixed.

- Witnessing improvement in my skills and abilities motivates me to keep pushing forward.
- Even when facing obstacles, I remain determined and resilient, always finding ways to overcome challenges.
- I welcome feedback from others because I understand its value in helping me grow. Constructive criticism serves as a guiding light to enhance my performance.
- The success of others inspires me to strive for greatness.
- I am a lifelong learner, continuously seeking new knowledge and experiences to broaden my horizons and expand my capabilities.
- Resilience is a core aspect of my personality.
- A positive outlook is my guiding principle.
- I focus on the process of growth and development, valuing every step I take toward my goals.

- I tend to get defensive when I receive feedback, as I don't want to acknowledge any weaknesses.
- The success of others sometimes makes me feel inadequate or envious.
- I avoid exposing my weaknesses to others, fearing it might lead to judgment.
- Setbacks and failures can be disheartening for me, leading to discouragement and sometimes even giving up on my goals.
- When I encounter obstacles, I tend to feel overwhelmed by the challenges ahead.
- My outlook can be pessimistic at times, and I may struggle to see the positive side of situations.
- I often focus on achieving immediate success rather than appreciating the process of growth and learning.
- I take failures personally, believing they reflect my weaknesses.

- I know that I can continuously develop and achieve great things with dedication and effort.
- When I encounter setbacks, I see them as temporary hurdles, not permanent roadblocks.
- I am self-motivated, constantly pushing myself to go beyond my comfort zone and challenge myself in new ways.
- I am open to trying new experiences and stepping outside my comfort zone.

- I may doubt my potential for growth and self-improvement, feeling limited by my current abilities.
- I believe that my talent determines my potential, and if I'm not naturally good at something, I may avoid trying it altogether.
- I tend to stick with familiar routines and situations, as stepping outside my comfort zone makes me uneasy.

Now that you've marked the situations you find yourself in most often, it's time to score yourself. Review the list again and count the marked points in each mindset set. Note the total number of marked examples for "Growth Mindset" and "Fixed Mindset."

———————— ————————

Growth Mindset   Fixed Mindset

If you have more marked examples in the "Growth Mindset" set, you predominantly exhibit a growth mindset in various areas of your life.
- If you have more marked examples in the "Fixed Mindset" set, you may lean towards a fixed mindset in certain aspects.

The time has come for you to look closer at your dominant mindset.

If you lean towards a growth mindset, celebrate your openness to challenges and opportunities for learning and growth. Think about how you can further embrace these qualities to continue improving.

If you are leaning towards a fixed mindset, consider this an exceptional opportunity to embrace growth and self-awareness. Don't be afraid to acknowledge the challenge ahead of you and use it as an opportunity to learn. Challenge yourself to shift your mindset, actively embrace obstacles, and learn from failures with determination. Try to keep a positive attitude and that setbacks are just learning experiences. Adopting this self-awareness and growth journey will unlock your potential and pave the way for continuous improvement.

Extra!

Take a moment to reflect on your choices.

- Are there specific examples that stand out to you? Take a moment to identify those that resonate most deeply with you.
- Do you relate more to one set of examples than the other? Consider which set of examples you feel a stronger connection with. Reflect on the patterns and themes you observe in your choices.
- Are there any surprises in your choices? Take note of any unexpected or contradictory responses. Sometimes, we lean towards different mindsets in various aspects of our lives.
- What do your choices reveal about your mindset in different areas of your life? Consider how the examples you resonate with reflect your attitudes and beliefs in various domains such as work, relationships, personal development, or facing challenges.
- How do your mindset choices impact your daily decisions and actions?
- Are there areas in your life where you want to cultivate a different mindset? Based on your reflections, identify areas where you might benefit from shifting your mindset towards growth or embracing more growth-oriented qualities.

- What steps can you take to develop a growth mindset further? Consider actionable strategies to nurture a growth-oriented approach in areas where you may lean towards a fixed mindset. Think about setting SMART goals, seeking support from others, and adopting a positive and resilient mindset.

10 Steps to Develop a Growth Mindset

It is truly beyond our imagination what the Growth Mindset can do. Our perspective on life determines how far we can go. If you don't believe me, look at Oprah. She emerged as a shining beacon of resilience and determination from a challenging childhood marked by poverty and adversity. Her journey from humble beginnings to becoming one of the most influential women in the world is a testament to the transformative power of embracing a growth mindset.

In the early 1980s, Oprah faced numerous obstacles, skepticism, and rejection from the media industry. Yet, rather than letting these setbacks define her, she learned, grew, and adapted.

Oprah's growth mindset was evident as she sought self-improvement and personal growth. She expanded her knowledge by immersing herself in learning opportunities, reading, and seeking mentorship from influential people. She didn't shy away from challenges but instead turned them into learning and growth opportunities.

Her commitment to a growth mindset was profoundly reflected in her groundbreaking talk show, "The Oprah Winfrey Show," where she fearlessly tackled pressing social issues and inspired millions with her authenticity and empathy. The open-mindedness and willingness to embrace change that characterized Oprah's show transformed it into a platform for fostering meaningful conversations and inspiring personal transformations.

Oprah's journey is a great inspiration for all of us who want to be better versions of ourselves. Before getting into the 10 recommendations you should consider to develop a Growth Mindset, I hope you are aware of the power of embracing this mindset. As we explore the 10 recommendations to develop a Growth Mindset, let's recognize the incredible power of embracing this mindset. It can genuinely lead to transformative personal and professional success.

So, how do we foster a growth mindset toward personal development? These are 10 simple ways I have discovered that help develop a growth mindset:

• Stop Comparing Yourself to Others

Often, we are too preoccupied with what others have rather than focusing on our own growth. Unfortunately, this hinders personal development because there's no room for growth when you're too busy comparing yourself to others.

• New Skills Require Failure and Practice

The more new skills you learn, the greater the possibility of failure. However, don't let failure demotivate you. Embrace these setbacks as excellent learning opportunities to continue improving.

- ## Learn from Your Mistakes

Mistakes allow us to reevaluate our beliefs and assumptions. We learn more from our failures than our successes, as failure compels us to question our methods and try something new. Don't be afraid of failure; it eventually leads to success.

- ## Utilize Feedback to Your Advantage

Receive criticism without taking offense. Remember that everyone has the right to their opinion, whether correct or fair. The crucial part is how you handle this feedback, not whether others agree with it or not.

- ## Work Towards Improvement Every Day

Be passionate about personal development. Find something new that interests you and see how far you can take it. We've already agreed that passion for life is essential for success, so don't let a fixed mindset hinder your growth. Focus on improvement rather than comfort, push your limits, and challenge the status quo.

- ## Never Settle for "Good Enough"

One of the most important mindsets to adopt is that you can always do better. Even if you've achieved something, there's still room for improvement. Celebrate small victories and keep pushing yourself to be even better.

- ## Don't Fear Failure; Embrace it as Feedback

The fear of failure can be a significant obstacle. Instead of being afraid, think of failure as a valuable tool to gain the feedback you need for improvement. If you accept failures, you can learn from them and easily escape your comfort zone. Failures are valuable lessons on the path to success, so why avoid them?

• Practice Mindfulness

Did you know your emotions can make or break you? Your way of thinking is influenced by your thoughts and the feelings tied to them. If you're anxious, depressed, or lacking motivation, practicing mindfulness can help.

• Accept What You Can't Control

Learn to accept things you cannot change if you want to improve! Realize that only you have control, which means there will always be barriers and obstacles in your path. The only difference between those who succeed and those who fail is how they deal with these inevitable challenges.

• Think of Your Weaknesses as Skills to be Practiced

You can't expect overnight improvement if you've spent years developing a fixed mindset. Think of your mindsets as skills that need practice, like learning to ride a bicycle. The more time and effort you put in, the better you'll become. It's okay if you're not where you want to be yet; with practice and dedication, you'll catch up.

I hope you can cultivate this unique mindset by following these simple tips. Remember, all it takes is the right mindset at the right moment to achieve success, so know that you can always do more than you believe are your limits.

In pursuing excellence, we often get caught up in external factors and overlook the most influential force: the power of self-motivation and personal growth. Embracing a growth mindset means recognizing that your abilities and talents are not fixed but rather capable of continuous improvement and development.

In the quest for success, never underestimate the transformative power of personal development. While external circumstances may fluctuate, your growth mindset will remain the driving force that propels you forward.

So, as you continue to pursue your goals, remember that **the most potent tool at your disposal is the commitment to work on yourself continually**. With every step you take towards personal growth, you will be inching closer to success in ways you never thought possible. Trust in your ability to adapt, evolve, and exceed your expectations.

Remember, success is not just a destination but a continuous evolution of who you are becoming.

Chapter 3

Key takeaways

- Carol Dweck's Mindset Theory categorizes beliefs about intelligence and abilities into fixed and growth mindsets.
- A growth mindset firmly believes in the potential for improvement and embraces challenges and failures as opportunities for learning and growth.
- A fixed mindset views abilities as fixed traits, leading to avoidance of challenges and a fear of failure.
- Understanding the characteristics of growth and fixed mindsets can help you recognize your dominant mindset and work towards developing a growth-oriented approach.
- Cultivating a growth mindset empowers you to take on challenges, embrace learning opportunities, and see effort and perseverance as the keys to success.
- Embracing a growth mindset can lead to continuous improvement, personal growth, and resilience in the face of obstacles.
- The 10 steps to develop a growth mindset include avoiding comparisons, learning from failures, utilizing feedback, working towards improvement, refusing to settle for mediocrity, embracing failure as feedback, practicing mindfulness, accepting what can't be controlled, seeing weaknesses as skills to be practiced, and understanding the journey of growth.
- The power of self-belief and personal growth is an influential force that propels you forward in the pursuit of success.

- Personal development is a continuous evolution, and by embracing a growth mindset, you can exceed your own expectations and achieve remarkable success.

BE A CATALYST!

"We cannot become what we need to be by remaining what we are."

– Max Depree

We shape our own futures, but that doesn't mean the opportunities that present themselves can't be our guides. In a sense, this book provides you with its own Choose Your Own Adventure question: Do you carry on blindly going through the motions, or do you decide it's time to take charge? You already had the motivation to do something different – that's why you picked up this book. But it could be that the guidance you find here is the catalyst for whatever you choose to do next.

You can be that catalyst for someone else. There's someone else like you out there, someone who knows there's something more for them but who needs a little help to get the ball rolling… and a few words from you could present exactly the opportunity they need to take a deep breath, dive in, and start taking control of their own destiny.

By leaving a review of this book on Amazon, you'll show that person (and many others like them) that we really do have the power to shape our future – and you'll show them exactly where they can find all the guidance they need to make it happen.

When someone's searching for information, it's reviews like yours that help them find what they're looking for… so the few minutes you spend doing this could quite literally help someone change their life. We have ultimate control, but the opportunities around us make it clear what we need to do.

Thank you for your support. As we'll see later in the book, embracing lifelong learning is going to be key to your success – and one of the things that helps us to learn and grow is reinforcing what we've discovered by sharing it with others. It's a win-win for everyone!

OVERCOME PROCRASTINATION AND PERFECTIONISM

"Don't let perfectionism become an excuse for never getting started."

- Marilu Henner

Have you ever felt like you're your own worst enemy in reaching your goals? There are two primary explanations for that: perfectionism and procrastination. Imagine them as those annoying speed bumps on your way to success. These are struggles that many of us face, and finding the key to overcoming them is the ultimate strategy for achieving significant success.

While perfectionism is defined as holding oneself or others to high standards, procrastination means putting off important tasks. **Despite their differences, both originate from a common underlying fear of making mistakes.** Generally, people struggle to accept they can mess up, making it harder to navigate the road. The key is accepting that mistakes can be made and finding the right balance between pushing yourself and knowing when to stop.

In this chapter, you will learn how to deal with perfectionism and procrastination. As you learn about these two terms, you will understand how they relate and affect your daily life together. The key is learning about yourself, your limits, and your challenges so you can push yourself to be your best version while caring for your well-being. As Albert Einstein once said,

"Once we accept our limits, we go beyond them."

Understanding Procrastination and Perfectionism

Procrastination has been an age-old challenge, pestering individuals throughout history. While not everyone falls victim to it, understanding and addressing this problem is crucial for personal growth and supporting others struggling with it.

Procrastination
Irrational tendency to delay tasks that should be completed
(Lay, 1986).

"Procrastination" finds its roots in the Latin words "pro," meaning "forward," and "crastinus," meaning "belonging to tomorrow." The well-known expression, "I'll get to it later," is a typical response from those who procrastinate, highlighting their tendency to delay tasks.

Taking long to complete assignments at school and work is an example of this delay phenomenon.

It is well known that procrastination has a long history, dating back to ancient times. Did you know that even the Egyptians recognized this unhealthy tendency to delay tasks? Hieroglyphic inscriptions that hinted at missed deadlines or delayed projects can be found amidst the grandeur of their historical records.

Studies show that procrastination has nothing to do with intelligence. Approximately 20-25% of the general population and nearly 70% of university students are procrastinators today. It has also been said that men seem to procrastinate slightly more than women.

Having said that, it is essential to understand that there is a difference between procrastination and strategic delay. Sometimes, people put off tasks because they genuinely don't have enough time or because they're taking a more relaxed approach rather than because they feel compelled to avoid the task.

Studies have demonstrated that procrastination adversely affects many aspects of life. For instance, Klingsieck, K. B. (2013) found that procrastination negatively impacts students' performance, anxiety levels, and stress levels. In light of the negative impact of procrastination on personal and academic success, various intervention programs have been designed to mitigate its effects.

To develop effective strategies to address procrastination, it is crucial to understand the root causes and the factors that lead to it. These triggers may include fear of failure or criticism, disassociation, low self-esteem, a tendency towards self-defeat, depression, attention deficit hyperactivity disorder (ADHD), difficulty focusing, and decision fatigue.

As you might imagine, the most common cause of procrastination is **perfectionism**. Simply put, procrastinators tend to be perfectionists, and vice versa.

How are perfectionism and procrastination linked?

Perfectionism
The wish for everything to be correct or perfect

Perfectionism is a multidimensional concept that incorporates both social and personal aspects. According to Hewinn and Flett, there is **self-oriented perfectionism** (high standards and motivation for the self to attain perfection), **other-oriented perfectionism** (tendency to expect perfection from others), and **socially prescribed perfectionism** (perception that other people expect oneself to be perfect).

Perfectionist personalities impose irrationally high standards on themselves and procrastinate because they do not believe they can meet them. **Basically, when individuals think they should be perfect, they may find it safer to procrastinate rather than take action and potentially face the judgment of failure.**

The perfectionism-procrastination puzzle

Let us take a closer look at the inner workings of this counterproductive cycle - a tapestry woven by our thoughts, emotions, and behaviors.

How Perfectionists Think

Perfectionists frequently find themselves on high alert, scrutinizing their performance for the slightest hint of inadequacy. Hypersensitivity manifests itself in attitudes like taking negative feedback personally and interpreting discomfort as a sign of incompetence when initiating a task.

A common problem for perfectionists is that they start thinking in ways that aren't helpful. Even though these thoughts are often not true, they feel like they are. Strangely, these thoughts make them feel more stressed and overwhelmed, which makes them feel less motivated. So, they end up delaying things because of these negative feelings. Some common ways they think are:

- All or Nothing Thinking: This entails striving for unattainable standards, like equating a score below 100% to personal failure. This unrealistic approach plants the seeds of stress and overwhelm, setting the stage for the loop.
- Catastrophic Thinking: They might blow minor problems out of proportion, like thinking that saying one wrong thing in a meeting will ruin their reputation. These exaggerated thoughts make them want to avoid things so they don't mess up.
- Mind Reading: They sometimes assume that others are harsh critics, like thinking that a boss will be harsh and call their work terrible. Their thoughts prevent them from showing their work to others.

What happens after they do something just reinforces the cycle. They might think they're only good when under pressure or believe their results don't show how good they are. Beliefs like these keep the process of trying to be perfect and then putting things off.

How perfectionists feel

Due to their habit of self-criticism, perfectionists suffer when their lofty expectations are not met. This mentality keeps them mired in a negative self-perception, which compounds their low self-esteem. Feelings of anxiety, guilt, overwhelm, doubt, and even depression can follow failure to meet their demanding standards.

Procrastination becomes the refuge of least resistance when these emotions become so intense.

How perfectionists behave

Ultimately, behavior is what links perfectionism and procrastination. In the realm of anxiety management, our fight-or-flight response activates when confronted with a challenge – in this case, a task demanding perfection. This flight response manifests in procrastination as a strategy to avoid the perceived threat of failure and the negative emotions that ensue. Common procrastination behaviors encompass

- Indecisiveness: Struggling to select an assignment topic, paralyzed by the need for the "perfect" option that guarantees a stellar presentation and top grades.
- Premature Surrender: Perfectionists often capitulate prematurely, opting to abandon efforts rather than risk failure, preferring the comfort of avoidance.

- Task Postponement: From avoiding the initiation of assignments to investing excessive hours in research without embarking on the actual task – all these strategies delay engagement. This evasion prevents grappling with potential imperfection.

While these procrastination strategies exacerbate psychological distress, they also uphold perfectionism's principles. Engaging in these behaviors prevents genuine learning experiences: Success is achieved, but a lingering thought of starting earlier (for example) would have led to even better results obscures true potential. In the event of failure, external factors like pressure or anxiety are conveniently attributed, safeguarding self-esteem while evading genuine self-assessment.

We become captured in a vicious cycle of perfectionism and procrastination, clouding our perception of what we are capable of and obstructing our growth as a result.

In other words, procrastination frequently emerges from the fear of not meeting exceptionally high standards or worrying about being criticized for imperfect outcomes. This connection suggests that if you are a perfectionist, you may delay tasks and responsibilities to avoid confronting the anxiety of potential failure or imperfection.

As you might imagine, procrastination and perfectionism hurt productivity and mental well-being. On the productivity front, it can lead to missed deadlines, reduced efficiency, and increased stress as tasks pile up and become more daunting.

Regarding mental well-being, the pressure to be perfect can take a toll on individuals' self-esteem and self-worth. A common belief among those struggling with procrastination and perfectionism is: "My achievements reflect my immense capabilities, thus boosting my self-worth." Paradoxically, it's precisely this mindset that often becomes a catalyst for eventual emotional strain. A dangerous cycle of self-judgment and discontent begins when one's worth is tied to constant achievement and flawless outcomes.

In addition, research has shown that perfectionist tendencies can significantly impact life satisfaction. A study conducted by Chang (2000) found that the perfectionist personality trait was associated with moderate adverse effects on life satisfaction. Perfectionist thoughts were identified as contributing to decreased life satisfaction, suggesting that the constant pursuit of perfection can hinder one's ability to find contentment and fulfillment.

Understanding how perfectionism and procrastination are connected reveals a lot about how we act and how it affects our work and happiness. This knowledge is your tool to stop the cycle of putting things off and find a better way to aim for greatness without feeling overwhelmed. So, as you move forward, remember this idea. It's like a map guiding you to get things done and feel good about it.

Take a moment to reflect on how perfectionism is impacting your life.

Identify three excessively high standards you have set for yourself (e.g. I have to be the best at doing my job)

1.

2.

3.

Standard 1:
Is this standard reasonable for me?

Standard 2:
Is this standard reasonable for me?

Standard 3:
Is this standard reasonable for me?

Are you caught up in the perfectionism-procrastination loop?

Many individuals find themselves entangled in this cycle, a seemingly never-ending dance between two opposing impulses. On one side, there's the relentless pursuit of perfection, driven by the desire to excel and achieve flawless outcomes. On the other, there's the tendency to delay tasks and actions, often due to the fear that they won't meet the impossibly high standards set by perfectionism.

This loop can be both frustrating and detrimental to personal growth and productivity. At first glance, striving for perfection might seem like an admirable trait. After all, who would want to avoid delivering impeccable results and showcasing their capabilities?

However, the dark side of perfectionism lies in the pressure it creates. The belief that anything less than perfection is unacceptable can lead to an overwhelming fear of making mistakes. This fear, in turn, fuels the procrastination side of the loop. Due to your fear that you'll fall short of your ideal, you hesitate to start tasks.

It is a vicious cycle where the fear of imperfection fuels procrastination, while procrastination reinforces feelings of inadequacy. You might wonder why you get trapped in this cycle. Is there a cause? Many factors contribute to this loop, including how we think, feel, and act. It is fuelled by overanalyzing feedback from external sources, catastrophic thinking, negative emotions, and behaviors like putting off a task or giving up if it seems too hard.

Thankfully, you can interrupt the procrastination loop by acknowledging the pressures of perfectionism and recognizing the triggers of procrastination. By accepting imperfections as a natural part of life, one can take calculated risks and learn from failures.

Small Steps, Big Wins: One is More Than Zero

Procrastination often stems from feeling overwhelmed when faced with a seemingly large task. The activity below will help you practice breaking tasks into the smallest achievable steps. Doing so lets you discover that even the most daunting tasks can become manageable and less intimidating.

Breaking Tasks into Minimum Steps

Choose a task from your to-do list that you've been postponing. It can be something as simple as doing the dishes, organizing your closet, or starting a project. Then, follow the steps below to break the task into its minimum components.

Task Selected:

_____

Step 1: Identify the Task

Write down your chosen task and acknowledge why you've been putting it off.

Task:

_____

Reason for Procrastination:

_____

Step 2: Break it Down

List the smallest, simplest steps required to complete the task. Each step should be so easy that you can complete it in a few minutes or less.

Smallest Steps:

1. _____

2. _____

3. _____

4. _____

5. _____

Step 3: Choose One Step

Select one of the smallest steps from your list. This is your starting point. Remember, the goal is to make it incredibly easy to start.

Chosen Step:

_____

Step 4: Take Action

Now, take action and complete the chosen step. Set a timer for 5 minutes if needed, but commit to finishing this small step.

Action Taken:

_____

Step 5: Reflect

After completing the chosen step, take a moment to reflect on your experience. How did it feel to take action on such a small task? Did it feel less intimidating than tackling the entire task at once?

Reflection:

_____

Extra: Repeat and Build

If you feel motivated, choose another small step from your list and complete it. If not, that's okay – you've still made progress! Over time, you can continue to build on these small steps to complete the entire task.

Additional Steps Taken:

_____

By completing this activity, you've successfully practiced breaking down a task into its smallest components and taking action. Remember that every small step counts and adds up to achieving your larger goals. Whenever you find yourself procrastinating in the future, use this approach to break tasks down and conquer procrastination.

When perfectionism and procrastination go too far: Analysis paralysis

Attempting to break free from the intricate loop caused by procrastination and perfectionism can sometimes be challenging. When that happens, a series of negative consequences can surface, leading to feelings of frustration and inaction. Among these consequences, "analysis paralysis" stands out.

Imagine you're trying to choose what to eat for breakfast or what movie to watch, but you get stuck because you think so much about all the options. You want everything to be perfect, so you keep thinking, but this can make you feel confused and unable to decide.

This is known as analysis paralysis, the inability to decide due to overthinking. It occurs when a person is confronted with too many decisions that are so important that over-analysis results in inaction.

This paralysis is closely connected to perfectionism. Often, people seek the best or "perfect" solution and fear making decisions that could result in erroneous outcomes. As a result of this fear, we tend to overanalyze every decision, seeking certainty that rarely exists.

When someone falls victim to Analysis Paralysis, they procrastinate until all the pieces come together perfectly, sometimes never happening. While postponing can temporarily relieve the pressure of perfection, it wastes valuable time and opportunities. As minutes turn into hours and hours into days, the window for progress narrows, and the fear of making the wrong choice intensifies.

Consequently, we end up in analysis paralysis, where overthinking becomes a heavy anchor that prevents us from moving forward. Believe it or not, this happens to companies too.

Many tech companies face analysis paralysis when developing new products. Trying to anticipate every possible feature or competitor response can result in delays and missed opportunities because they spend too much time and money on perfection.

An excellent example of this is the release of Microsoft Windows Vista. The release was highly anticipated in 2007, but numerous delays and performance problems plagued it. In an attempt to incorporate multiple features and enhancements, Microsoft created a bloated and complex operating system. Overanalyzing features and an extensive development process contributed to its poor reception.

Also, customers may experience analysis paralysis when faced with thousands of choices during their shopping trip. In a study done in 2014, results showed that consumers are known to postpone their buying decision when spoilt for choices; when fewer options exist, deals are closed more quickly. The vast options overwhelm them and cause them to become paralyzed.

In essence, analysis paralysis showcases how the interplay of perfectionism and procrastination can lead to unexpected consequences – both in our personal lives and in the business realm. Recognizing this dynamic can empower us to make more informed decisions, striking a balance between deliberation and action and steering clear of the paralysis that stems from excessive overthinking.

To conquer this paralysis, we must address our tendency to overanalyze everything. But the question remains: how can we achieve this?

Tips to Overcome Analysis Paralysis

Overcoming analysis paralysis is within your reach. Let's explore some actionable strategies to help you make decisions more confidently and efficiently.

 Accepting imperfections

In a world that often glorifies flawlessness, encouraging a shift in mindset towards accepting flaws is a powerful tool to combat analysis paralysis. When we embrace imperfections, we can escape the suffocating grip of overthinking and are empowered to take action. By understanding that perfection is unattainable and that mistakes are natural, we can liberate ourselves from the fear of failure. This mindset shift cultivates resilience, creativity, and a greater sense of freedom, ultimately leading to more fulfilled and meaningful pursuits. The ability to accept imperfection frees you from analysis paralysis.

The benefits of learning from failures and mistakes.

Mistakes and failures are not setbacks but stepping stones to growth and success. When we view these experiences as opportunities to learn and improve, analysis paralysis disappears. Each misstep becomes a valuable lesson, guiding us toward more informed decisions. Learning from mistakes fosters adaptability and a deeper understanding of ourselves and our endeavors. We can ensure continuous growth and advancement by accepting failures as part of the journey.

Progress over perfection.

Progress over perfection is a mantra that can break the cycle of overthinking and indecision. Choosing progress means taking steps forward, even if they are imperfect. It involves setting achievable goals and continuously improving upon them. The focus is on just starting instead of worrying about whether the step is good enough, which will help us overcome procrastination.

Incorporating these three principles—accepting imperfections, learning from mistakes, and valuing progress—can liberate you from the analysis paralysis trap.

Taking lessons from failure

In our journey toward personal and professional success, the inevitability of failure becomes evident. Initially, it can feel like a daunting obstacle. However, as illuminated by Chapter 3, when we approach failure with the right mindset, it shifts from a setback into a valuable platform for learning and growth. Much like a mirror, failure reveals your vulnerabilities and areas needing improvement. This reflective process presents a golden opportunity for skill enhancement and personal development, emphasizing the significance of acknowledging our limitations.

In summary, ignoring perfectionism and procrastination makes achieving personal growth difficult. You need to know how these psychological processes impact you to manage them successfully. Balancing ambition with self-compassion becomes the key to navigating these psychological challenges effectively. Accepting your imperfections and deriving wisdom from your mistakes empowers you to transcend the limitations set by perfectionism and drive forward with newfound determination.

Einstein's words, "Once we accept our limits, we go beyond them," resonate deeply here. The journey is inevitably beset with roadblocks, yet your understanding of perfectionism and procrastination guides you to navigate it more smoothly. Active goal-setting, time management, and self-discipline are crucial to conquer procrastination. When combined with practical strategies and guidance from mentors and peers, breaking free from inertia and fostering productivity becomes a genuine possibility.

The transformative power of embracing self-compassion cannot be understated. The pursuit of excellence and growth lies not in the pursuit of perfection but in continuous dedication to becoming a better version of yourself.

This culminating understanding allows you to unlock your full potential. Your journey isn't about achieving perfection but embracing improvement, one step at a time.

Chapter 4

Key takeaways

- Our dreams and potential can only be achieved if we overcome the obstacles we face.

- Perfectionism sets unrealistically high standards, while procrastination leads to delaying tasks. Despite their differences, perfectionism and procrastination share an underlying fear of making mistakes. Perfectionists dread imperfection and potential criticism, while procrastinators postpone tasks due to the anxiety associated with possible failure.

- Recognizing the link between perfectionism and procrastination is crucial for navigating challenges effectively. Understanding how these two forces interact and impact our actions can help us break free from their grip and achieve our goals.

- Analysis paralysis, overthinking, and indecision can be alleviated by embracing imperfections. Accepting that perfection is unattainable allows us to make decisions confidently, breaking free from the cycle of overthinking.

- Failures and mistakes are not setbacks but growth opportunities. We break free of analysis paralysis by seeing these experiences as lessons to learn. Each misstep becomes a valuable lesson guiding us toward more informed decisions. Failure reveals weaknesses and areas for improvement. In acknowledging our shortcomings, we gain a sense of self-awareness that enables us to actively pursue personal growth and development.

- We can cultivate resilience, creativity, and freedom by shifting our perspective to accept imperfections. If we embrace the idea that growth is borne out of trial and error, we will be empowered to move forward without fear of failure as we progress toward our goals.
- Conquering procrastination requires setting clear, realistic goals. Breaking larger tasks into manageable steps and establishing timelines provides direction and focus, combating the urge to delay.

BUILD RESILIENCE AND MENTAL TOUGHNESS

"Life is 10% what happens to us and 90% how we react to it."

- Charles R. Swindoll

Anyone who has been to the sea knows how quickly it can change from moment to moment. There are times when it appears to be a tranquil mirror, its calm surface reflecting the serenity of the world around it. Yet, it can be transformed into a tempestuous force in the blink of an eye. As strong winds blow, waves grow bigger and crash intensely against the shore.

Life, much like the sea, is an ever-changing and unpredictable journey. As you set sail on a journey of personal growth and self-discovery, you might feel like a lone sailor navigating a vast ocean of possibilities. You set sail with the desire to become the best version of yourself, steering towards your goals with unwavering determination. However, as the sea sometimes surprises you with sudden storms, you may also be faced with unexpected challenges and frustrations.

Your unshakable foundations will be tested in these moments of uncertainty and adversity. Like a seasoned sailor, you must learn to adjust your sails, embracing life's changing winds and tides with resilience and mental toughness. This chapter is your compass, guiding you through the stormy waters and teaching you to find strength in the face of the unpredictable.

When facing setbacks, two things can happen. You can feel defeated and lost, or you can embrace the waves of discomfort as opportunities for growth. **Just as the sea shapes the coastline with every powerful surge, each challenge molds and strengthens your character.** The journey to personal growth isn't about avoiding rough waters; it's about learning how to navigate them effectively.

Sailors are made, not born. They become skilled through practice and with the help of the right tools. For this reason, within this chapter, you'll find strategies to enhance your resilience, enabling you to remain firm in your purpose even when the seas around you are fierce. You'll discover techniques to manage stress and stay focused amidst the turmoil, much like a skilled sailor navigating through a raging storm.

External Adversities: An Unpredictable Terrain

The concept of "adversities" has been examined by experts over the years, offering various perspectives and definitions. One author who excels in this field is Angela Duckworth. With her emphasis on grit and resilience, her insights are very compelling.

When I first came across Angela Duckworth's ideas, they resonated deeply, allowing me to understand better how to deal with adversity.

Grit, as defined by Duckworth, represents a blend of passion and unwavering perseverance. It embodies a relentless determination to persevere, even when faced with formidable challenges. Grit goes beyond fleeting motivation; it's the tendency to sustain interest in and effort toward very long-term goals.

External adversities, as elucidated by Angela Duckworth, encompass an extensive array of unforeseen obstacles and setbacks that weave into the fabric of your life. These adversities extend beyond your direct control, encompassing events such as natural disasters, economic downturns, health crises, and unforeseen impediments. **They are unanticipated disruptions that life hurls your way, challenging your plans and testing your strength.**

External adversities

Grit

Extensive array of unforeseen obstacles and setbacks that weave into the fabric of our lives.	**Tendency to sustain interest in and effort toward very long-term goals.**

Think about events that can instantly shake us to our core, such as an earthquake and a market crash. Imagine how you'd handle unexpected health challenges or obstacles that pop up out of nowhere. As Duckworth points out, we cannot predict these misfortunes; their magnitude can significantly impact our lives.

External adversities span a vast spectrum, often without rhyme or reason. Consider these scenarios:

- **Natural Disasters:** A sudden earthquake, a raging wildfire, or an unexpected flood can shatter our sense of security. These phenomena are the very embodiment of nature's indifference to our plans.

- **Economic Downturns:** Market crashes and financial downturns can wipe out fortunes and alter destinies, irrespective of meticulous financial planning.

- **Health Challenges:** A sudden illness or an unforeseen medical condition can throw our lives into disarray, despite our best efforts to sustain a well-balanced, healthy lifestyle.

- **Unforeseen Obstacles:** A missed flight, a computer crash erasing months of work, or a sudden family emergency can disrupt our carefully orchestrated routines.

- **Relationship Dynamics:** The actions and decisions of others can introduce chaos into our lives, affecting relationships, partnerships, and interactions in ways we cannot predict.

- **Global Events:** Societal shifts, political changes, and cultural movements can shape our world, altering the landscape without our consent.

In essence, Duckworth's exploration of external adversities serves as a reminder that life's journey is a complex dance of uncontrollable circumstances. In her work, she highlights the importance of cultivating grit and resilience as essential tools for navigating this rugged terrain. Through the lens of grit, we better understand how people overcome adversities and emerge stronger and more determined.

The Grit & Resilience Formula

The interplay between grit, resilience, and a growth mindset, has been a subject of contemplation and study. Angela Duckworth introduced intriguing insights into this dynamic in a 2013 TED talk (which is well worth watching). In her perspective, a growth mindset serves as a foundation for cultivating grit. Since you already know much about growth mindset, let's dive deeper into the unknown: grit and resilience.

At its core, the crucial role of grit and resilience becomes evident in navigating life's hurdles. Just as a ship relies on a strong structure and clear direction to navigate rough waters, those armed with grit and resilience chart a steady course through life's difficulties. This partnership isn't just a vague idea; it highlights a powerful reality: the fusion of these qualities propels us towards growth even when facing challenging situations.

By cultivating these noble qualities, we bring persistence, courage, and adaptability into the picture. Together, these virtues form an unyielding shield that empowers you to overcome challenges and nurture a thriving growth mindset.

The pace at which we cultivate resilience and grit varies from person to person, and cultural nuances play a critical role in that process. As the American Psychological Association highlighted, the following strategies can lay the foundation for these attributes:

Ten Paths to Foster Grit and Resilience

1. **Social Bonds:** If you are not a social person, becoming more social (i.e., purposely connecting with others) can help.

2. **Response Mastery:** Get control over how you respond to the adverse events you experience.

3. **Accept Change:** "The only constant in life is change," said the Greek philosopher Heraclitus. Embrace change. The inability to accept things that we cannot change is a futile pursuit.

4. **Kaizen Approach:** Apply the Kaizen principle to your goals. Start with the smallest component related to the larger, long-term goal.

5. **Decisive Action:** Commit to making decisions when you find yourself in a tough situation. There is no room for half-hearted actions.

6. **Learn from your suffering:** We can learn a lot about ourselves when we struggle through a bad experience. How have our relationships grown? How have we gained strength or perspective?

7. **Forget negative self-talk.** Trust that you know yourself better than anyone and have the intelligence and power to make forthright decisions.

8. **Temporal Perspective.** Bad things will happen eventually; try to think about them from a lifelong perspective. In the grand scheme of your life, how significant is this situation? Looking back at past events, how much or how little do they affect your life now?

9. **Practice optimism.** This is not a denial of the bad. It is an acknowledgment of the good and what is possible in your life.

10. **Approach well-being holistically.** Self-Compassion, Fitness, Learning, and Laughter: A holistic approach nourishes both grit and resilience.

Now that we've taken a closer look at Duckworth's ideas about how to deal with life's challenges, let's explore some practical steps for handling chaos when it shows up in your life. It's important to have a game plan for those moments. And for that, we'll shift our focus to a saying that holds valuable advice.

The Chaos Out There: Embracing the Limits of Control

Even if you don't find solace in matters of faith, you've likely encountered the timeless wisdom encapsulated in the **serenity prayer**. It is a mantra that often finds its way into support groups, resonating as people seek recovery and personal growth. If you're unfamiliar with it, let me introduce you:

"Grant me the serenity to accept the things I cannot change, courage to change the things I can, and wisdom to know the difference."

In these simple yet meaningful words, we find a map to understand the twists and turns of life. As life's chaos inevitably presents itself, it provides a solid foundation for surviving and thriving when chaos arrives.

Embracing the Unchangeable

"Grant me the serenity to accept the things I cannot change…" There's a big difference between giving up and accepting. When challenges show up, sometimes the best way to go is acceptance. This does not mean surrendering but finding calmness in accepting what you can't change. Just like the sky makes its colors without us doing anything, there's a place where things happen on their own. Rain falls whenever it wants, and the tides follow their own rules. **Some things are beyond our control, and that's ok.**

In this way of thinking, you're invited to discover the peace that comes when you let go of trying to control everything. It's like a humble hug, a way to let go of the heavy burden of trying to control every part of life. Being at peace with the fact that we can't control everything is about finding comfort in what can't be changed.

Cultivating Courageous Change

"...courage to change the things I can..." With these words, the prayer extends an empowering invitation, opposite to the one before. Some situations are an invitation to step boldly into the arena of influence. It's a reminder that there are aspects of life's canvas upon which your brushstrokes can leave a mark. **While you may not command the winds, you can adjust your sails.**

This part gets us moving and tells us to stand strong. It asks us to be brave and face the problems we can change. Sometimes, it's necessary to be courageous, try new things, dream big, and break down the things stopping us from making a difference.

Discerning the Difference

"...and wisdom to know the difference." This last part of the prayer gives us a special kind of knowledge. And it's, in my opinion, the most valuable piece of advice you can get to face life's challenges. **It's**

essential to recognize that each situation is unique, so we must identify which situations we can influence and which come into our lives to teach us acceptance. A fulfilling life, even if it includes suffering, requires learning to recognize the two kinds of situations described before.

This wisdom is like the captain of your ship, helping you sail through stormy waters. It's like a guide that shows you the best way to go, considering what you can do and what you can't. **It points you towards where your hard work makes the most difference, where your energy can make things better.** And it stops you from crashing into the things you can't change, keeping you strong for the battles you can actually do something about.

Take a moment to think about difficult situations you've faced lately. Here are some ideas:

- You had to adapt to a sudden restructuring in your job role, which brought uncertainty and adjustments.
- Dealing with an unexpected illness, you had to deal with medical appointments, treatments, and recovery.
- The recent market crash impacted your investments, causing financial stress and reevaluating your financial goals.
- Missing an important flight due to unforeseen circumstances, you had to rearrange travel plans.
- You experienced conflicts in personal relationships, leading to emotional distress and challenging conversations.
- Changes in the learning environment or remote education posed challenges in staying engaged and focused.
- Your neighborhood underwent urban development, affecting your daily routines and surroundings.

- Facing public transportation disruptions, you had to find alternative routes to get around.
- Societal shifts and political changes prompted you to reevaluate your opinions and beliefs.
- Rapid technological advancements require learning new skills to stay relevant in your field.
- _____
  _____
- _____
  _____
- _____
  _____
- _____
  _____

1. Embracing the Unchangeable

"Grant me the serenity to accept the things I cannot change..."

Think about the situations you've listed above; which of those were beyond your control? Reflect on times in your life when you tried to control something you couldn't. How did it make you feel? Write down your thoughts on this phrase.

2. Cultivating Courageous Change

"...courage to change the things I can change..."

Consider the examples you've mentioned earlier. Among them, identify instances that were within your power to influence. Reflect on the times when you actively attempted to change something you had control over. How did you approach these situations, and what were the outcomes? Jot down your reflections on this aspect of the prayer.

3. Cultivating Wisdom

"...and wisdom to know the difference."

Reflect on the challenging situations you've listed. Think about a recent decision where you had to choose between trying to change something or accepting it. How did you navigate these moments when you had to discern between circumstances you could change and those beyond your control? Were there instances where you struggled to recognize the difference? Write down your thoughts and insights about gaining wisdom in knowing when to accept and when to take action.

Connecting the Dots

Look at your notes and notice how each part connects to the next. Take a moment to reflect on the wisdom you've gained from each part of the serenity prayer.

Write down one action you can take based on each part of the prayer. For example, "I will practice acceptance in situations beyond my control," "I will take a brave step towards positive change," and "I will pause and consider my choices before reacting."

Just as sailors navigate the open sea with tools and guidance, you can navigate life's journey with the wisdom you've gathered. By embracing acceptance, cultivating courage, and discerning your choices, you become a skilled sailor of your own life.

The serenity prayer teaches us something important about facing challenging situations we can't control. First, we need to be smart about what to do. Should we accept things as they are or try to make them better? Knowing these answers helps when we're in a difficult spot.

Once you've figured out what needs to be done, it's time to take action. Yet, there is a significant challenge that often goes unnoticed: stress. **Stress has a way of showing up when things are tough, and it can throw you off course.**

When you're working hard to handle a situation, stress can sneak in and cause problems. It can affect how you think, how you feel, and even how you make decisions. It's like an unexpected obstacle that gets in your way.

By understanding how stress works and managing its effects, you can stay focused, make better choices, and stay on track as you tackle challenges. So, as you navigate tough times, keeping stress in check becomes critical to building resilience and achieving your goals.

The Art of Responding, Not Reacting

When the storm clouds of adversity gather on the horizon, it's natural to feel a surge of stress and anxiety. External adversities can profoundly impact our performance across various facets of life.

This link between stressful situations and how we react is tied to something our body does naturally: cortisol. This is a hormone that our body makes when we're stressed. It's like an automatic reaction when we're faced with things we can't control. Cortisol helps our body prepare to deal with these challenges by making changes inside us.

Cortisol has historically played a crucial role in human survival, aiding reactions to threats from predators and environmental dangers. However, a study by Mather et al. (2012) revealed that heightened cortisol levels can impact decision-making processes. Researchers observed that elevated cortisol levels were associated with impulsive and risky decision-making.

Simply put, our stress response can cloud our judgment, hinder our decision-making abilities, and even undermine our overall well-being. But here's the twist: while you may not have direct control over what causes the trouble, you possess immense power over how you respond to it.

As a result, it is crucial to recognize stress cues and manage cortisol effects to make well-considered choices in the face of challenges. And here's where experts come in.

Psychologists and specialists in this field teach us how to cope with stress without losing focus on our goals and values. The World Health Organization (WHO) has compiled an illustrated guide titled "Doing What Matters in Times of Stress," featuring the expertise of seasoned psychologist Russ Harris.

This guide presents a comprehensive approach rooted in Acceptance and Commitment Therapy (ACT), a scientifically supported method for effectively managing stress and navigating through challenging times. How to handle stress like a pro begins with mastering these principles.

Grounding	Grounding involves anchoring oneself in the present moment, fostering mindfulness, and reducing the influence of distressing thoughts. By connecting with your senses and surroundings, you can shift your focus away from worries about the past or future, promoting a sense of stability and calmness.

Unhooking

Unhooking refers to the process of disentangling from unhelpful thoughts, emotions, and beliefs that can trap you in cycles of negativity. Instead of getting caught up in these internal experiences, ACT encourages you to observe them from a distance and let them come and go without judgment or attachment.

Acting on Your Values

This concept underscores the importance of identifying your core values and aligning your actions with them. Living in accordance with your values, even in the face of challenges, can cultivate a sense of purpose and fulfillment, contributing to a meaningful and authentic life.

Making Room

Making room involves creating space for uncomfortable emotions, thoughts, and sensations rather than trying to avoid or suppress them. Acknowledging and accepting these experiences can reduce their power over you and develop greater emotional resilience.

Engaging

Engaging refers to actively participating in activities and experiences that bring joy, fulfillment, and a sense of connection. Engaging in meaningful actions can enhance your overall well-being, foster positive emotions, and divert your focus from distressing thoughts.

Being Kind

Practicing self-compassion and kindness towards yourself is crucial in ACT. Treating yourself with understanding and gentleness, especially during times of adversity, can help reduce self-criticism, enhance your emotional well-being, and promote a healthier relationship with yourself.

It's unrealistic to expect constant happiness. While difficulties are unpleasant, they are crucial to assessing resilience. To cultivate your inner strength, you must embrace the full spectrum of human experience, both pleasant and unpleasant.

It is because of this that special tools are required. Acceptance, courage, and wisdom are necessary for navigating life's turbulent seas. In the same way a sailor adapts to changing winds and tides, you can cultivate resilience and mental toughness to overcome whatever obstacles life puts in your way.

The serenity prayer serves as a guiding compass, helping you to discern the difference between the controllable and the uncontrollable. However, wisdom alone may not be enough when emotions cloud your judgment. To stay on track toward our goals, different strategies are needed when stress appears.

You can face adversity with authenticity and grace by anchoring yourself in the present, detaching from negative thoughts, aligning your actions with your values, embracing discomfort, taking purposeful action, and practicing self-compassion. As a sailor's expertise grows over time, so will your ability to face challenges with resilience, mental toughness, and a growth-oriented mindset.

Remember, the measure of a man is not solely in his ability to control the uncontrollable but in his capacity to respond to the unchangeable with grace, resilience, and unwavering determination.

Chapter 5

Key takeaways

- Life is unpredictable, and facing challenges is part of personal growth.
- Embrace acceptance and courage to navigate life's changing winds with resilience and mental toughness.
- External adversities encompass unforeseen obstacles, like natural disasters, economic downturns, and health crises.
- Grit, defined by Angela Duckworth, blends passion and perseverance for long-term goals.
- Resilience and a growth mindset are essential for navigating life's challenges effectively.
- Strategies for building grit and resilience include social bonds, response mastery, accepting change, and practicing optimism.
- The serenity prayer guides us to accept the uncontrollable, make courageous changes, and discern wisely.
- Cortisol, produced during stress, can affect decision-making; managing stress is crucial for clear choices.
- Acceptance and Commitment Therapy (ACT) principles include grounding, unhooking, acting on values, making room, engaging, and self-kindness.
- Cultivate inner strength by embracing life's full spectrum, using tools like acceptance, courage, wisdom, and the serenity prayer.

SURROUND YOURSELF WITH SUPPORTIVE RELATIONSHIPS

"The most important things in life are the connections you make with others."

– Tom Ford

Almost everyone has enjoyed a football game at one point or another. It's definitely worth a try if you haven't already. The experience of watching a great football play, like "The Catch" from Joe Montana to Dwight Clark, is unforgettable. On the field, football players aren't just individuals; they're a cohesive unit that works towards a shared purpose. Beyond a perfect spiral pass and an acrobatic catch, teammates exchange unspoken words of encouragement, demonstrate empathetic understanding, and jointly celebrate minor triumphs and monumental victories. In sports where teamwork and strategy are paramount, supportive relationships are essential.

Just as each player contributes to the 49ers' success on the gridiron, our relationships with people who uplift, inspire, and bolster us play an equally vital role in our personal growth. **To flourish holistically, we must surround ourselves with positive relationships and**

unwavering support, ultimately contributing to our well-being. It is undeniable that the relationships we have in our lives play a crucial role in strengthening our journeys.

Being surrounded by the right people in adversity can make us resilient, propel us towards our aspirations, and equip us to deal with day-to-day challenges. **These supportive connections, whether a friend cheering us on, a mentor offering guidance, or a colleague sharing a reassuring smile, cultivate a sense of trust and bolster our self-assurance.** The success of the 49ers on the field is a direct result of their exceptional teamwork, mirroring how our triumphs in life's grand game are shaped by our intertwining with people who provide encouragement and support.

The chances are that you have encountered people who have left you feeling down and bad about yourself at some point. As there are people who can bring a smile to your face, there are also those who may unintentionally send a cloud of sadness your way. Learning to identify these different types of people is vital. You have the power to build the relationships you want and let go of those that bring you down. We don't just need people. We need the right people.

Hellen Keller once said: "Alone, we can do so little; together, we can accomplish so much." Success and making our way in the world are all about people; we need positive interactions and guidance. For this reason, throughout this chapter, you will explore the many benefits of supportive relationships and how they promote emotional well-being and contribute to potential development.

Building a Network of Supportive Relationships

Being surrounded by the right people can make all the difference. Supportive relationships are based on encouragement, listening, and transparency. Unfortunately, not all relationships share those characteristics. Because of this, it is crucial to distinguish between those that make your life better and those that drain your energy. Many mental health experts have studied this topic over the years. In particular, Marian Rojas Estapé stands out for her clear and accessible framework explaining the art of choosing a social circle.

Vitamin People

How familiar are you with vitamins? We could define them as health encapsulated in little pills. These tiny capsules of vitality can improve your health and improve your life. Vitamins are not meant to treat diseases but to improve general health and well-being.

In an intriguing parallel, Marian Rojas Estapé, a distinguished psychiatrist from Spain, employs the term "Vitamin People" to refer to people whose company enriches our lives. In the way that vitamins bolster health, some people make life more fulfilling. Conversely, other people might cause our cortisol levels to rise (as we've seen previously, this is related to stress). Luckily, Vitamin people promote well-being by releasing oxytocin, which protects the body from the harmful effects of stress.

Oxytocin is a hormone that plays a vital role in interpersonal bonds. A hug, laughing with friends, and many other things trigger oxytocin secretion. When oxytocin levels increase, cortisol levels decrease.

A growing body of research emphasizes the importance of well-founded relationships. When you're in a tough spot, the perfect hug can lower your cortisol; a trusting look can motivate you to overcome a challenge, and encouraging words can help you feel less alone.

Here are some characteristics of vitamin people:

1. **Empathy:** When you truly understand where others are coming from and step into their shoes, your connections flourish. This empathy makes your relationships feel more profound and more meaningful.

2. **Trust:** When you're someone others can rely on without hesitation, your relationships reach a whole new level. This trust makes your connections more robust and more genuine.

3. **Patience:** If you can roll with the punches and not let little mistakes bother you, your relationships become smoother. This patience helps you maintain a sense of ease in your connections.

4. **Optimism:** Maintaining a positive outlook on life can be a game-changer in your relationships. Focusing on the good and keeping negativity at bay adds an extra dose of happiness to your connections.

5. **Generosity:** When you're ready to go the extra mile, whether with your time, money, or kindness, your relationships deepen. This generosity cements bonds and makes your connections more solid.

6. **Humility:** Being humble and genuinely happy for others' successes without feeling threatened is a beautiful quality. This humility brings authenticity and harmony to your relationships.

When building better relationships, remember that the key is to do two things at once. First, **be the kind of person you'd love to have around:** empathetic, trustworthy, patient, optimistic, generous, and humble. Your positive vibe will create a ripple effect of goodness in your environment. Second, **don't underestimate the power of surrounding yourself with "vitamin people."** Identifying and connecting with those who share these qualities ensures you're immersed in a circle of positivity, lifting each other higher. So, embrace the balance of embodying these traits and finding them in others because that's where the actual transformation of your relationships begins.

Cortisol people

Conversely, some individuals trigger the release of cortisol in our bodies. These individuals, though perhaps not intentionally, can create an environment that raises our stress levels and leaves us feeling uneasy. Just as some people radiate positivity and happiness, others can unknowingly evoke stress and anxiety, impacting our well-being in ways we might not even realize.

Cortisol, commonly known as the "stress hormone," can surge when we're faced with challenging or threatening situations or when negative emotions appear.

The key to understanding this kind of person is to learn that their effect on others is a cortisol intoxication; they aren't toxic in themselves.

When they are present, or even just thought of, we are taken out of our comfort zone, deeply disturbed, saddened, irritated, and above all, we go into alert mode. So, when we're around such people, our sympathetic nervous system gets activated, the alert state kicks in, and cortisol starts secreting.

You might wonder, how can I recognize a "cortisol person" in my life?

It's not easy, that's for sure. A specific behavior or comment doesn't necessarily make a person harmful. We need to be attentive to repetitive behaviors or severe actions.

Cortisol people possess many characteristics, and you may share some of them. According to Dr. Rojas Estapé, many types of people may increase cortisol levels. Here are some of them.

The selfish one

This type needs to be the center of attention in every conversation. Being empathetic is not in their everyday language. They may struggle in listening and focusing on someone other than themselves. Living near a selfish type can be tiring because they want to be constantly reminded of their greatness.

The negative one

These are people who see the glass as half empty. They have a dramatic and pessimistic view of their surroundings. They tend to be angry at anything or anyone; it could be you, the temperature, the food, the traffic, the government, and, in general, the world. If you're close to them, you'll notice that you feel uncomfortable, insecure, and anxious.

The envious one

Toxic people are prone to envy. Whenever others succeed, they must criticize and humiliate them. It is here that contempt, insults, and humiliation are born. To avoid generating rejection from others, you might tend to hide your successes unconsciously as a defensive measure.

The victim

Their narrative is characterized by drama, and they readily adopt the role of victims in any situation they encounter. In this way, they manipulate those around them by causing feelings of guilt. They take advantage of your kindness and time, using various situations to seek favors or receive gifts and minimize their contributions.

The critic

You know those who always have something negative to say about others? People often enter the world of easy criticism when they feel unfulfilled, insecure, or empty. Gossip (a form of criticism) is often seen as a great way to connect with others. There is no doubt that this is incorrect. While you might think that you've found common ground when laughing together about someone, this shallow and unfruitful conversation doesn't make you better.

Two things might happen because of surrounding yourself with critics: Internal and external criticism. The first, internal criticism, can be very damaging to the body since how we talk to ourselves directly affects how we feel.

On the other hand, you might also engage in external criticism. How you communicate with others has a double harmful effect: it harms you and poisons the environment and the physiological balance of those around you.

Listed above are a few types of people who can cause stress. To begin your journey in supportive relationships, you must understand and identify the kind of people you are surrounding yourself with and if they are making your journey easier or more difficult.

Pause for a moment and reflect on who you choose to surround yourself with. Take a moment to jot down a few names that come to mind. Sort them into these two distinct categories as you go. With this simple exercise, you can identify the people who contribute positively to your life and those who might inadvertently cause you stress or negativity. As you identify these patterns, you're taking a proactive step toward nurturing healthier relationships and creating a more supportive and harmonious environment.

Vitamin people	Cortisol people

The advantages of surrounding yourself with positive influences

There are a lot of benefits that come with surrounding yourself with positive influences. In a study conducted in 2018, researchers delved into the impact of interpersonal dynamics on personal growth. Often viewed as a consequence of individual attributes, personal growth was explored through an innovative lens of relationships.

The investigation revealed intriguing insights: Individuals influenced by supportive connections displayed choices favoring personal growth opportunities. Intriguingly, this effect was mediated by nurturing self-confidence – a transformative aspect stimulated by interactions with supportive individuals.

In essence, this study illuminates the vital role of interpersonal connections in nurturing personal growth. It underscores that cultivating supportive relationships enhances immediate well-being and catalyzes the sustained and transformative personal development journey.

• Vitamin people motivate, uplift, and inspire you.

Supportive relationships are essential. There are several ways in which they provide motivation, create an atmosphere of inspiration, and offer moments of enlightenment. Imagine embarking on a new fitness journey. A supportive workout partner who cheers you on, celebrates your progress, and encourages you during challenging moments can be a powerful motivator. Their presence fuels your determination to push your limits and achieve your health goals. Having the right people on your side allows you to pursue your dreams and become better versions of yourself.

Positivity is contagious. You naturally adopt a similar mindset when surrounded by optimistic and enthusiastic people. By nurturing positivity, you cultivate resilience and problem-solving skills. This sparks an inner drive to confront life head-on, embracing whatever it brings. In this process, personal growth becomes an organic outcome.

• When you are with the right people, you grow.

This isn't limited to adulthood; it's something inherent that we can nurture from childhood. A child who receives consistent support and feels secure gains the freedom to explore the world and experience substantial growth. This foundation sparks curiosity, confidence, emotional well-being, and resilience. They embrace new challenges, develop independence, and cultivate a positive mindset. This environment nurtures immediate growth and fosters the skills and attitudes needed for a fulfilling and resilient future.

Just like plants need water and sun to grow, we need healthy relationships. They play a pivotal role in fostering personal growth and facilitating the achievement of goals. Becoming better at your work is more rewarding when you surround yourself with people who exude optimism, encouragement, and constructive guidance.

Vitamin people foster self-confidence. As you feel empowered by people who believe in you, you can set ambitious goals and pursue them with determination.

However, it doesn't stop there; vitamin people can provide valuable insights and perspectives. You benefit from their ideas, alternative views, and constructive feedback as you refine your approach to reaching your goals.

Finally, celebrating achievements becomes a shared joy in the presence of vitamin people. They appreciate the milestones you achieve, reinforcing your sense of accomplishment and reminding you how far you've come. This positive reinforcement fuels your determination to reach even greater heights.

- **Having supportive relationships during challenging times is vital to make them more manageable and bearable.**

When surrounded by people who radiate optimism, empathy, and unwavering support, adversity becomes less daunting.

Firstly, they serve as a source of emotional strength. Their encouraging words and genuine compassion remind you that you are not alone in your struggles. You feel less isolated and depressed when they offer understanding ear or comforting advice, which strengthens your sense of resilience emotionally.

Moreover, vitamin people provide practical support. Whether it's lending a helping hand, offering resources, or simply being there to share the load, their presence can ease the burdens that come with difficult times. This support network reinforces the notion that you can rely on others for assistance, reducing overwhelming feelings and fostering a sense of unity.

How do we build supportive relationships?

To build supportive relationships, it is essential to consider your attitude toward others. In this intricate dance of connection, looking inward and considering how you interact with those around you is as important as observing what others do. **Nurturing meaningful connections requires effort.** Here are a few things to consider:

1. **Communication is key:** Effective communication lays the foundation of any meaningful relationship. It involves not just talking but actively listening, understanding, and empathizing with one another. Transparent and honest conversations

foster understanding, prevent misunderstandings, and build trust. Open lines of communication allow for the exchange of thoughts, feelings, and ideas, strengthening relationships and making them supportive.

2. **Share vulnerability:** Vulnerability is the gateway to authenticity and deeper connections. Opening up about our fears, struggles, and insecurities allows others to see our true selves. By sharing our weaknesses, we create an environment of trust and understanding where both parties feel safe to express their genuine feelings. This mutual openness fosters a stronger bond and promotes empathy, ultimately enhancing the quality of the relationship.

3. **Be reliable and available:** Reliability and availability demonstrate your commitment and investment in the specific bond you have. Being there for someone when they need you, whether for advice, a listening ear, or assistance, showcases your dedication. Consistently showing up and keeping your promises builds trust and reinforces the idea that you're a dependable source of support.

4. **Goals and values must be shared:** Aligning goals and values with someone creates a sense of common purpose. When you share similar aspirations and principles, you are more likely to support and motivate each other in pursuing those goals. Shared values provide a strong moral foundation for the relationship, ensuring that decisions and actions are in harmony. The shared goals and values synergy strengthens the connection and propels both people toward growth.

5. **Celebrate each other's successes:** Celebrating each other's successes cultivates an atmosphere of positivity and encouragement. When you genuinely rejoice in another person's achievements, you reinforce their sense of accomplishment and worth. Recognizing one another's successes fosters mutual admiration and inspires continued efforts toward personal growth and success.

Extra! Now that you've learned the importance of building supportive relationships, let's put these insights into action. Take a moment to think about one relationship that could be made more supportive in your life. It could be a friend, family member, coworker, or anyone you interact with regularly.

- Reflect on Your Attitude: Take a moment to reflect on how you approach your interactions with the person you've chosen. Are you generally positive and empathetic, or do you find yourself being critical or distant? Write down a few keywords that describe your typical attitude toward this person.

- Communication Check: Reach out to the chosen person and initiate a conversation. Practice active listening by genuinely paying attention to what they're saying. Respond with empathy and understanding, showing you value their thoughts and feelings.

- Share a Vulnerability: In your conversation, take a brave step and share something about yourself that you don't usually talk about. It could be a fear, a challenge, or something you're working on improving. This vulnerability will likely encourage them to open up as well.

- Offer Your Support: Let the person know that you're there to support them. Ask if there's anything they need assistance with or if they'd like to share something they're dealing with. Your willingness to be available demonstrates your commitment to the relationship.

- Discuss Goals and Values: If possible, during your conversation, explore each other's goals and values. Do you have any common aspirations or principles? Discuss how you can encourage and support each other in achieving these goals. If this is not possible, take some time to reflect on this point on your own.

- Celebrate Success: If the person you're talking to shares a recent success, genuinely celebrate it. Offer your congratulations and express your admiration for their achievements. This positive reinforcement reinforces the idea that you're in their corner. Consider reaching out to someone else who has recently achieved success in their life and express your enthusiasm for them.

Different types of supportive relationships: Mentors

Mentoring originated in ancient Greece as a way to impart important values to young men. During this process, young people learned a trade by shadowing a master artisan. In a mentoring relationship, the mentee learns by observation and example from loosely defined, informal collegial associations to structured, formal partnerships between expert and novice mentors, where each develops professionally.

Regarding your professional and personal growth, mentors are essential and are part of what we call "supportive relationships." Along the way, you will run into people who will teach you a lot about yourself and how to make it to the top.

However, before we delve into mentor/apprentice learning, we must realize that your relationship with friends and loved ones differs from that with a mentor. Both are pretty important because of this difference.

A mentor is like a model or light you follow through the tunnel, while family and friends show you love and support. Mentors greatly influence you, so you tend to pay attention to their opinions more.

There are a few things that are specific to this type of relationship, "mentoring principles" described by William Hogue and Ernest Pringle.

1. **Agree on confidentiality.** Confidentiality is essential for building trust between participants. It is unlikely that a relationship will reach its full potential without the ability to speak freely as the situation requires.

2. **Commit to honesty.** Both parties need to be honest about what they hope to gain from the relationship and their vision for how to get there. Even if the feedback is critical, they should be prepared to offer frank criticism.

3. **Listen and learn.** When both members feel their viewpoints are heard and respected, mutual benefit and honesty can be achieved. Mentors, especially, must remember that the relationship isn't about them. It is essential for mentees to feel empowered and appreciated and not intimidated or made to feel their views are not valued.

4. **Lead by example.** Actions create the most lasting impression.

5. **Be flexible.** It might help for a mentoring relationship to have defined goals, but the process may be just as necessary—or even more so—than the purposes.

Having a mentor has several valuable advantages that foster personal and professional development. They offer guidance and insights from their experiences, helping mentees make informed decisions and set attainable goals.

They share practical knowledge and real-world perspectives beyond traditional education, enhancing mentees' understanding of their field. Mentors often have well-established networks, which allows mentees to connect with industry professionals, potential collaborators, and job opportunities.

Through constructive feedback and encouragement, mentors help mentees build confidence, overcome weaknesses, and develop new skills. Also, they provide accountability and motivation, ensuring that mentees stay focused on their goals through regular check-ins and goal-setting.

In conclusion, having a mentor is a pathway to accelerated growth, knowledge transfer, and increased self-confidence, making it a valuable investment in one's personal and professional journey.

Extra!

Mentoring: Getting started

Take a moment to reflect on your current situation. Are you currently in a mentorship role, either as a mentor or a mentee? Consider how the principles above apply to your current experiences.

If you're not currently involved in a mentorship, consider whether you would like to be mentored by someone. Identify the areas in your personal or professional life where you could benefit from guidance and support.

Seek a Mentor

If you desire to be mentored, consider people with the knowledge and skills you want to acquire. Think about professionals or people in your network who could offer valuable insights in those areas.

Reach out to potential mentors and express your interest in being mentored. Explain why you believe their guidance would be beneficial to you. Be open to their response and willingness to mentor you.

Consider Becoming a Mentor

Similarly, consider whether there are people in your life who could benefit from your experiences and insights. Reflect on individuals who value your guidance in their personal or professional growth.

If you're open to the idea of being a mentor, approach the individuals you've identified and express your willingness to share your knowledge and support. Explain how your experience aligns with their needs.

After completing these reflections, consider taking action based on your insights. Whether seeking mentorship or considering being a mentor, make the necessary steps to initiate these supportive connections.

The people we choose to have around can make a big difference in our lives. They help us when things are tough, guide us towards our goals, and make us feel better when things are hard. These relationships, whether friends, mentors, or colleagues, make us feel more confident and trusting.

You've probably heard the saying, "Teamwork makes the dream work." It's as simple as that. When we work together and support each other, we can accomplish more.

Just like a football team needs strong relationships to win, we need positive and uplifting connections to help us succeed and reach our goals. These connections give us the energy, motivation, and advice to overcome challenges and achieve what we want.

Similar to how plants need care to grow, we need good relationships to thrive. These relationships, like sunlight, water, and soil, help us grow. Every talk, smile, and moment we share adds to our story. By being kind, understanding, and connected, we build a garden of relationships that make our journey better. In the same way plants make the world more colorful, our connections make life richer for everyone.

Chapter 6

Key takeaways

- Supportive relationships in sports and life, offering encouragement, understanding, and celebrations. Positive relationships with people who inspire, motivate, and support us are vital for personal growth.
- Surrounding yourself with positive influences boosts resilience, motivation, and coping skills. Helen Keller's quote emphasizes the strength of collective effort. Positive influences promote self-confidence, personal growth, and optimism.
- Key steps to building supportive relationships: communication, vulnerability, reliability, shared goals/values, and celebrating successes.
- "Vitamin people" uplift, and "Cortisol people" cause stress. Characteristics of vitamin people: empathy, trust, patience, optimism, generosity, humility. Recognizing cortisol people: selfish, negative, envious, victim mindset.
- "Vitamin people" enhance oxytocin secretion, reducing stress and promoting emotional well-being. Toxic people increase cortisol secretion, causing stress and discomfort in relationships.
- Mentoring originates from ancient Greece and involves meaningful commitment. Mentors provide guidance, knowledge, networking, insights, and practical support for personal and professional growth and accountability. Mentoring is an essential part of supportive relationships.,. Friends/family and mentors are two different kinds of relationships.

- Principles of effective mentoring: confidentiality, honesty, listening, leading by example, and flexibility.

EMBRACE LIFELONG LEARNING WITH MINDFULNESS

"Live as if you were to die tomorrow. Learn as if you were to live forever."

— *Mahatma Gandhi*

As in the last minutes of a game, getting to the final chapter of this book might make you feel flooded with adrenaline and excitement. It's not a random occurrence that this is the moment I've chosen to introduce the concept of **lifelong growth**. With the tools mindfulness gives us, we can channel that vibrant energy into a nonstop growth process.

Similar to how athletes give their all in the final minutes of a game, I hope you are here engaging the 7th step wholeheartedly, embracing the value of continuous learning and personal growth.

Before diving into the final step, I'd like you to take a moment to breathe deeply. Inhale slowly, and as you do, let your focus settle on the feelings inside you. It's like tuning into a soft murmur of emotions in your head. There is no need to do anything special with these feelings. Just let them be there, like visitors you're paying attention to.

Which emotions do you experience? Perhaps you feel anxious, and your heart beats faster. That's anticipation, and it's okay if you're sensing that. It could also be that you are tired after a long work day. Whatever you're feeling is ok. Breathe deeply and let those feelings flow. Feelings are like the different weather patterns in an extensive landscape, each adding color to your inner world.

Before you turn the page – both in this book and your own life – you have a chance to look at these feelings with kindness. You're not trying to change them or push them away. Instead, imagine them like leaves gently moving in a calm stream. And when you breathe out, think about letting go of these feelings, just like you'd release a leaf into the water.

This act of noticing and then letting go is like having a quiet chat with yourself. You're saying it's okay to feel your feelings without judging them. You're appreciating the different shades of your emotions, like seeing all the colors in a painting. And as you take these deep breaths and let go, you're getting ready to step into what's ahead with a clear mind.

So, as you take a breath and exhale, you're starting this journey by giving yourself the space to just be. You're opening the door to what's next with a sense of calm, like the feeling after a good conversation. Congratulations! Having taken the first step towards mindfulness, you're ready to explore what this chapter holds with an open heart and mind. This simple act demonstrates that there's always room to learn something new, even in the quiet moments of self-reflection.

In a world that perpetually evolves, the ability to learn, adapt, and grow has become more than a choice; it's a necessity. In this rapidly changing society, lifelong learning is an important concept that guides us towards continuous personal and professional development. By exploring lifelong learning's qualities and its profound connection with mindfulness, we will discover a way to a purposeful and enriched life.

Understanding Lifelong Learning

Not long ago, experts believed that after our teenage years, our ability to learn declined to the point of being incapable of learning new skills. It's a good thing they were proved wrong because today, we know the human brain can learn and adapt to new situations until it dies.

This profound revelation led to the concept of Lifelong Growth. Today, we know we are equipped with the ability and actively encouraged to acquire new skills and knowledge throughout our lives. Substantial evidence suggests that consistently improving our repertoire of skills is crucial to our mental health and quality of life.

Just as regular physical exercise keeps your body fit and agile, engaging in continuous mental stimulation bolsters your brain's capacity and keeps it sharp. Additionally, acquiring new skills contributes significantly to your emotional and psychological well-being by boosting your sense of accomplishment and self-efficacy.

As you master new crafts or understand complex subjects, you reinforce a sense of accomplishment and purpose, releasing endorphins. This sense of accomplishment, in turn, acts as a potent antidote to the stagnation that can sometimes creep into your routine.

Essentially, the Lifelong Learning philosophy has created a new era of personal development where we constantly have the opportunity to learn and expand our horizons. Embracing this philosophy means adapting to our society's continuous changes and nurturing our own growth. This shift in perspective encourages us to approach each day as a chance to discover, evolve, and remain curious, ultimately leading to a fulfilling, vibrant, and endlessly rewarding life.

The avenues of learning are limitless, far extending the traditional classroom setting. Learning does not follow a single path; multiple activities, circumstances, and the wisdom of others influence it.

"Sharpen the Saw"

Stephen Covey's writings offer invaluable guidance to those seeking personal and professional development. An interesting metaphor he uses to refer to lifelong growth and personal effectiveness is "sharpening the saw." Simply put, with this expression, he underscores the critical importance of self-renewal in four dimensions: physical, mental, emotional, and spiritual. **Just as a well-maintained saw can cut with precision, our lives can operate at their best when we invest in our well-being.**

Your body deserves care and attention through exercise, proper nutrition, and rest. Your mind craves stimulation and growth through learning and new challenges. Nurture your emotional well-being by fostering meaningful connections and developing your emotional intelligence. Lastly, feed your spirit by exploring your sense of purpose and connection to something greater.

This holistic approach to renewal ensures that you stay sharp, adaptable, and resilient on your lifelong growth journey, allowing you to bring your best selves to every endeavor consistently.

As with preparing soil before planting, continuous growth involves working on yourself to facilitate the process of developing skills throughout your life. **In the same way that you nurture and till the soil for it to become fertile, cultivating the right qualities forms the foundation for your continuous learning journey.**

Qualities of a Lifelong Learner

Let's start with a simple truth: We're always learning, every day. Some people make the most of it, while others miss out. The best way to make the most of this journey is to identify the traits that make lifelong learners shine.

 Open mind

An open-minded person is willing to listen to and consider other people's ideas and suggestions. A person like this knows there are many ways of doing things and is open to attending to different viewpoints.

As a lifelong learner, this quality becomes essential. Imagine your current understanding as a confined box, a comfortable and familiar space. As a lifelong learner, you can step out of this box and explore the entire world.

 Curiosity

Being a lifelong learner requires an insatiable thirst for knowledge. Without a burning desire to learn, progress stays stagnant. It is, therefore, essential to be curious. Curiosity drives you to keep asking questions and learning new things.

With curiosity as your guide, you'll embark on a journey where you're always looking for new insights and where every corner of knowledge is a source of inspiration. When you nurture your curiosity, you pave the way for continuous evolution, ensuring every step you take is filled with wonder and learning.

Resilience

The last quality is mental flexibility. Resilience is defined as a person who can withstand or recover quickly from difficult conditions. Yes! We've talked about resilience before. It's all about engaging, taking control of the situation, and seeing stress more as an opportunity than a threat.

A resilient mind, however, is not easy to achieve. Luckily, many skills discussed in the book are key to building resilience. Moreover, a mindful approach can effectively round out your toolkit for cultivating resilience.

When was the last time you tried something new?

_____

_____

What are the advantages of Lifelong Growth?

As far as personal self-improvement is concerned, lifelong learning offers many advantages. Here are some key benefits of adopting a continuous learning mindset:

- **Enhanced Adaptability:** Lifelong Learning equips you with the tools to navigate the ever-evolving landscape of life, career, and relationships. It enables you to stay flexible and adaptable, ensuring that you're well-prepared to face any challenges that come your way.

- **Career Advancement:** Constantly updating your skill set through learning keeps you ahead in the competitive job market. This translates to increased job satisfaction, better opportunities, and the potential for higher earnings.

- **Physical Well-Being:** Continuously learning and adapting can improve physical health. Regular exercise, exploring nutritious diets, and discovering new ways to care for your body contribute to improved overall well-being.

- **Mental Clarity and Focus:** Lifelong growth enhances mental clarity and focus. This cognitive sharpening allows you to excel in learning, daily tasks, and problem-solving.

- **Emotional Resilience:** Acquiring new skills and knowledge boosts self-confidence and emotional resilience. These qualities help you handle stress and adversity better, improving your emotional well-being.

- **Purpose and Direction:** Lifelong learning often leads to discovering new passions and interests, providing a greater sense of purpose in life. This newfound sense of direction can motivate you to pursue your goals and dreams.

- **Physical Fitness**: Engaging in new physical activities or sports can improve your fitness level. It's an enjoyable way to maintain your body and stay active, promoting a longer and healthier life.

- **Social Connections:** Lifelong learning can extend beyond the individual. Joining classes, groups, or communities centered around your interests can expand your social circle and enrich your social life.

- **Personal Fulfillment and Happiness:** Continuously striving for personal growth brings a deep sense of fulfillment and happiness. Accomplishing goals and overcoming challenges provide a continuous source of joy.

- **Role Model and Mentorship**: By embracing lifelong growth, you become a role model for others, especially the younger generation. Your dedication to self-improvement inspires them to follow a similar path, creating a positive cycle of growth and mentorship.

As you can see, the benefits of Lifelong Growth are both practical and profound. Continually seeking knowledge, honing skills, and embracing personal growth are essential to creating a more fulfilling and successful life. It is a journey that demonstrates the resilience, adaptability, and confidence that defines someone who is multifaceted and empowered.

Extra!

Here are simple steps to becoming a lifelong learner by nurturing a sense of curiosity and seeking out knowledge on your own:

- Read more books per year
- Listen to podcasts, and watch documentaries (you can learn whatever you want on YouTube, for free).
- Invest in continuous education and short courses.
- Stay attentive to news and market trends.
- Always engage in conversations with mentors and other professionals with more experience than you.

As with everything in life, our ability to learn and evolve hinges on our perspective. The lens through which we view our growth potential can empower or limit us. Embracing a growth mindset, as psychologist Carol Dweck advocates, opens doors to endless possibilities. It encourages us to see challenges as opportunities, setbacks as stepping stones, and effort as the path to mastery.

You might wonder where to start as you prepare for a self-improvement journey. Maybe you're contemplating enrolling in an art class, pursuing your real estate license, or going back to the gym. I can't tell you what's best for you directly, but I can offer you a crucial tool you might be missing: Mindfulness. Self-awareness is the key to making authentic and effective choices.

Fusing these powerful philosophies (life-long growth and mindfulness) propels you toward genuine personal development, ensuring your path is well-defined, deeply meaningful, and gratifying.

The Synergy between Mindfulness and Lifelong Growth

You might wonder, "What does mindfulness have to do with the path of lifelong learning?" Well, being aware of and engaging with your reality empowers you. Rather than being a passive observer, you become a proactive participant in your own life.

Imagine you were born with a crystal-clear lens through which you saw the world as it truly is. Over time, this lens becomes clouded by various factors: upbringing, cultural influences, past experiences, and relationships. As layers accumulate, they obscure your vision, distorting reality. A subtle criticism might feel like a harsh attack, or a golden opportunity might go unnoticed.

In this context, mindfulness serves as a gentle but effective lens-cleaning process. It allows you to wipe away the accumulated dust and grime, that is, the biases, assumptions, and conditioned responses that have formed over time. Practicing mindfulness might not result in immediate changes, but it alters how you interpret and understand the world around you. This, in time, has profound effects on your reality.

Now, let's merge this idea with the concept of continuous learning. By striving to learn new things throughout your life, you're gradually replacing your old lens with new, polished ones. These new lenses offer distinct viewpoints that enrich your understanding. In the same way, a kaleidoscope offers different patterns with each turn; your evolving perspectives provide new insights into the world around you.

Simply put, continuous learning equips you with a growing toolbox of knowledge and skills. This toolbox not only offers practical benefits but also shapes your mindset.

When combined, mindfulness and continuous learning become allies in refining your perspective. Mindfulness enhances your ability to observe your experiences without immediately reacting, and continuous learning broadens your mental toolkit, enabling you to comprehend situations from different perspectives.

In essence, mindfulness and continuous learning work together to elevate perception. **By intertwining these practices, you're continually polishing your lenses and expanding your collection** of viewpoints. This heightened perception, in turn, enhances your ability to learn and grow. Mindfulness sensitizes you to the present moment, and constantly learning new things offers the tools and knowledge necessary for genuine personal evolution.

A brief overview of mindfulness and its benefits

With a history spanning centuries, mindfulness has recently come into the spotlight for its potential to promote well-being and personal growth. At its core, mindfulness encompasses three fundamental elements that work in harmony to create a transformative experience: awareness, acceptance, and investigation.

- **Awareness:** The cornerstone of mindfulness lies in being keenly aware of your external and internal surroundings. It's about being fully present in the moment, acknowledging the sensations within your body, and understanding the currents of your thoughts and emotions. This heightened awareness gives you a deeper connection to your inner workings and the world around you.
- **Acceptance:** The concept of acceptance within mindfulness invites you to become a non-judgmental observer of your own experience. Even when faced with uncomfortable thoughts and emotions during a mindfulness practice, the principle of acceptance encourages you to acknowledge them without attempting to alter or suppress them. This practice of non-reactive observation fosters a gentle, compassionate relationship with your thoughts and feelings.
- **Investigation:** Delving further into mindfulness, you encounter the investigation aspect. This involves recognizing multiple sensations simultaneously and describing them in intricate detail. Think of it as painting a vivid picture of your current state of being through

words. This exploration extends beyond the physical sensations to encompass your mental processes. It's an opportunity to uncover the complex landscape of your mind, uncovering hidden layers and gaining insights into your own thought patterns.

Contrary to popular belief, you don't need to be a seasoned Buddhist monk to reap its benefits. **Mindfulness is a practical and straightforward technique that can significantly enhance your life.** It involves channeling your focus into what you're doing and why you're doing it, a practice that steers your mind away from wandering and keeps it engaged in the present moment.

Mindfulness has shown numerous benefits. It can reduce stress, improve mental health, enhance emotional regulation, increase focus and attention, aid pain management, and boost overall well-being. These benefits underscore the value of incorporating mindfulness into daily life for improved mental, emotional, and physical health.

As you can see, the positive impact of mindfulness is profound. It's not just about sitting still; it's a powerful tool for personal transformation. Through awareness, acceptance, and investigation, you cultivate a profound connection to yourself, your emotions, and your environment. In a world often marked by distractions and stressors, mindfulness offers a sanctuary of presence, enabling you to navigate life's challenges with greater clarity, calmness, and insight.

Extra!

Integrating Mindfulness and Learning

- Before delving into the text, ground yourself with a few deep breaths. Read slowly, absorbing each word's significance. Pause periodically to reflect on connections to your prior knowledge. Make a conscious effort to absorb every word in the book rather than simply shoving it in your face.

- When talking to someone, try listening to them, truly listen to them. Put your distraction away and leave the response for later. You will understand that you can learn a lot more in this way. Also, respond thoughtfully, pausing before replying. Embrace differing perspectives without instant judgment.

- Use all your senses when observing. Observe intricate details - colors, textures, shapes. Consider how your observation stirred your emotions. In this way, the thing that enters your eyes will mean a lot to you.

- Every time you learn, give yourself time to reflect. Consider how new information aligns with existing knowledge.

- In new subjects, maintain curiosity and wonder. Embrace unfamiliarity with an open mind. Resist haste, savoring every facet of the learning process.

- And lastly, if you have time, take time to meditate. People are often talking about this; you have undoubtedly heard about it.

- Always engage in conversations with mentors and other professionals with more experience than you.

Mindful Growth

Mindful growth is not a destination but a continuous journey. It's about evolving and adapting as you gain new insights and experiences. This journey is marked by self-awareness, compassion, resilience, and an unwavering commitment to personal betterment. This is what you need to know if you want to master Mindful Growth.

The Power of Awareness: At the heart of mindful growth lies the power of awareness. This is not a passive state but an active, present-moment engagement with your thoughts, emotions, and actions. It involves observing your inner landscape without judgment and with a gentle curiosity. By doing so, you gain insights into your habits, tendencies, and areas for improvement.

Intentional Self-Examination: Mindful growth invites you to look closer at your beliefs, values, and aspirations. It's a process of intentional self-examination where you question the assumptions and narratives that shape your lives.

Embracing Change: Mindfulness encourages you to embrace change as an integral part of growth. Rather than resisting or fearing change, you learn to navigate it with grace and resilience. This acceptance of impermanence allows you to let go of the past, be present at the moment, and welcome the possibilities of the future.

Balancing Inner and Outer Growth: Mindful growth is not solely an inner journey. It also extends to your external experiences and interactions. It emphasizes the importance of nurturing meaningful relationships, practicing empathy, and contributing positively to our communities. This balance between inner and outer growth enriches your life. It allows you to make a meaningful impact on the world around you.

Cultivating Patience and Compassion: Personal growth is a lifelong endeavor, and mindful growth acknowledges this reality. It fosters patience and self-compassion, reminding you that setbacks and challenges are part of the process. Instead of viewing them as failures, you see them as opportunities for learning and refinement.

Living with Purpose: Mindful growth encourages you to identify and align with your life's purpose. When mindful of your values and passions, you can make choices that resonate with your authentic selves. This sense of purpose provides a guiding light on your journey and infuses your actions with meaning. Reflecting on your values is a vital part of living with purpose.

Self-Reflection and Alignment in Lifelong Growth

Pausing to contemplate your path and setting a deliberate and purposeful course for your future stands as the foundation for fostering healthy and sustainable growth.

The rush of everyday life can make it easy to lose sight of the profound personal development journey you are embarking on. Taking the time to reflect and contemplate allows you to pause and truly appreciate how far you've come, the challenges you've overcome, and the lessons you've gleaned along the way.

Integrating mindfulness and reflection into your life is like setting the stage for an ongoing, captivating journey of personal development that aligns with your core values. It's about unlocking the full extent of your potential and staying intrinsically motivated to evolve continuously.

Self-reflection allows you to tap into the reservoir of your aspirations and reignite the passion that propels you forward. During self-reflection, you reaffirm your "why." You reconnect with the core reasons driving your pursuits and reassess your paths. This contemplative process is akin to a navigator checking their compass, ensuring alignment with their true north.

As you reflect on your journey, you discover twice as much as you thought you knew. Reflecting on your progress and growth across these dimensions empowers you to refine your personal development journey. By dedicating time to nurture your physical, spiritual, mental, and emotional well-being, you create a foundation for continuous growth and learning.

Just as sharpening a saw ensures efficient cutting, nurturing these dimensions ensures your ability to navigate challenges and thrive in your lifelong development journey.

Extra!

Tips for sustaining motivation through self-reflection

- **Make time for self-reflection:** Set aside regular, uninterrupted time for self-reflection. Whether it's a few minutes at the end of the day or a longer session each week, designate this time as sacred for self-exploration.
- **Create a quiet space:** Find a peaceful environment to detach from distractions. This allows you to immerse yourself fully in the process of reflection without external interruptions.
- **Keep a journal:** Maintain a reflective journal where you record your thoughts, insights, and experiences. Writing helps you articulate your feelings and thoughts, making the reflection process more structured and meaningful.
- **Start with open-ended questions:** Begin your reflection with open-ended questions like "What did I learn today?" or "What challenges did I face?" These prompts invite deeper exploration and contemplation.
- **Focus on specific areas:** Concentrate your reflection on particular aspects of your life, such as personal goals, relationships, career, or personal growth. Trying to tackle all areas in one sitting is just too overwhelming.
- **Review goals and progress:** Regularly review your goals and track your progress. Assess how far you've come, what you've achieved, and any adjustments needed to align with your objectives.

Mindful growth is a profound approach to personal evolution that thrives on the union of awareness, intention, and adaptability. It calls you to engage with life deliberately, consciously, and openly, fostering deeper connections with yourself and the world. It is a path of self-discovery and transformation that empowers you to lead more authentic, purpose-driven, and fulfilling lives.

Ultimately, it's vital to remember the wisdom of the famous saying: "Appreciate the small things, for someday you might see that they were the most important." This idea captures the heart of self-improvement through being mindful. The path to becoming a better person is made up of these mindful moments, like little strokes on the painting of our lives.

While you work on knowing yourself better, building meaningful relationships, and staying true to your authentic self, you'll realize the little, everyday things shape your personal growth and happiness. In the big picture of life, the mindfulness and purpose you bring to each moment truly define your journey of personal growth.

Chapter 7

Key takeaways

- Lifelong growth is a continuous journey of learning and personal development that requires mindfulness and self-awareness.
- Embracing mindfulness allows you to channel your energy into a nonstop growth process, ensuring your personal development is intentional and meaningful.
- Continuous learning and growth are essential in a rapidly changing world, and they contribute to mental, emotional, and physical well-being.
- Stephen Covey's metaphor of "sharpening the saw" emphasizes the importance of self-renewal in four dimensions: physical, mental, emotional, and spiritual.
- Qualities of a lifelong learner include open-mindedness, curiosity, and resilience.
- Lifelong growth offers various benefits, such as enhanced adaptability, career advancement, physical well-being, mental clarity, emotional resilience, and personal fulfillment.
- Integrating mindfulness with lifelong growth enhances self-awareness and the ability to perceive and adapt to life's challenges.
- Mindfulness comprises awareness, acceptance, and investigation and offers numerous benefits, including reduced stress, improved mental health, enhanced emotional regulation, increased focus, and overall well-being.

- Integrating mindfulness and learning involves being present in your activities, listening actively, using all your senses, reflecting on new information, and staying curious.
- Mindful growth is an ongoing journey that focuses on self-awareness, compassion, resilience, embracing change, and living with purpose.
- Self-reflection is essential for sustaining motivation and aligning your personal development journey with your core values.
- Mindful growth encourages you to nurture physical, spiritual, mental, and emotional well-being, ensuring your ability to thrive in your lifelong development journey.

INSPIRE ANOTHER READER!

Your entire view of the world changes when you realize you have this level of control, and it's hard to understand when you see others feeling powerless. Take a moment to spread the word and help more people shape their own destiny.

By simply sharing your honest opinion of this book and a little about your story, you'll inspire new readers to take their own life-changing journeys.

MAKE A LASTING IMPRESSION!

Thank you so much for your support. Now, set forth! You have an incredible adventure ahead of you.

CONCLUSION

A new film has recently graced our screens, leaving us in awe of the incredible narrative surrounding the Williams Sisters. "King Richard" is a powerful and inspirational movie that explores the extraordinary journey of Richard Williams, the father of tennis icons Venus and Serena Williams. At the heart of this captivating story is the quote that encapsulates the essence of his character and determination: **"I love effort. That's my happy place."** This quote is a testament to Richard Williams' unwavering belief in the power of hard work, dedication, and perseverance—a belief I also hold.

Just as a sculptor meticulously chisels away at a rough block of stone, your path consists of countless small steps. The first chisel strike might seem inconsequential, barely altering the stone's appearance. However, with each precise strike, the form evolves. Over time, just as the stone transforms into a work of art, your life is shaped by these seemingly minor actions, accumulating like each chisel strike, gradually sculpting a masterpiece. The genuine essence of achieving greatness lies in the accumulation of these intentional, incremental efforts.

To conclude, I have found navigating the seven steps to attaining a self-motivation mindset to be an incredibly transformative and personal journey. Just like King Richard in his famous quote, "I love effort. That's my happy place," I've discovered the joy of sharing the profound truth in embracing effort as a source of personal growth and fulfillment.

We've explored the power of passion, intention, the art of self-belief, the significance of perseverance, adaptability, resilience, and the beauty of self-reflection. I want to finish by sharing with you the joy of gratitude. I hope each step has been a revelation and a reminder that your future is not set in stone but crafted through your choices and actions.

Effort is more than just a means to an end; it's a place where joy, personal growth, and self-discovery flourish. I hope this notion stays with you as you prepare to close this book and embark on your own path. Know that I am walking beside you as a fellow traveler, and your journey, like mine, is a testament to your remarkable potential for growth and change.

Remember, in the pursuit of excellence, there is no finish line. Instead, see every achievement as a stepping stone to the next, each milestone as proof of your dedication and progress.

In moments of doubt, recall the sculptor and the stone, the image of transformation through consistent, purposeful effort. When faced with challenges, look within yourself and remember the fire of your passions. When setting your course, let the compass of mindful learning guide you toward perpetual growth.

My own journey, marked by moments of self-doubt and self-assurance, has only strengthened my belief in the transformative power of these steps. Through my effort, reflection, and resilience, I've found the courage to share this wisdom with you. So please, if this book has resonated with you, consider leaving a review on Amazon.

With the knowledge and tools we've uncovered together, I encourage you to move forward with the conviction that you have the power to shape your destiny. Embrace the beauty of effort as your ally, and let it guide you as you persistently pursue your dreams. Your unique journey begins now, and I look forward to seeing the incredible future you will create for yourself.

REFERENCES

Introduction

- Tschohl, J. (2018). Giving It Your Best Shot. Agency Sales, 48(4), 28

Chapter 1

- Amemiya, R., & Sakairi, Y. (2019). The effects of passion and mindfulness on the intrinsic motivation of Japanese athletes. Personality and Individual Differences, 142, 132-138.
- Csikszentmihalyi, M. (1996). Flow: The psychology of optimal experience.
- Harris, R. (2022). The happiness trap: How to stop struggling and start living. Shambhala Publications.
- Datta, A. (2014, October 1). Fighting to the finish. Alive, 384, 25.
- Kruger, J., & Dunning, D. (1999). Unskilled and unaware of it: How difficulties in recognizing one's own incompetence lead to inflated self-assessments. Journal of Personality and Social Psychology, 77(6), 1121-1134.

- Vallerand, R. J. (2010). On passion for life activities: The Dualistic Model of Passion. Advances in Experimental Social Psychology, 42, 97-193.
- Vallerand, R. J., Blanchard, C. M., Mageau, G. A., Koestner, R., Ratelle, C., Léonard, M., ... & Lesage, F. (2003). Les passions de l'âme: On obsessive and harmonious passion. Journal of Personality and Social Psychology, 85(4), 756-767. Vallerand, R. J., Blanchard, C., Mageau, G. A., Koestner, R., Ratelle, C., Léonard, M., ... Marsolais, J. (2003). Les passions de l'âme: On obsessive and harmonious passion. Journal of Personality and Social Psychology, 85(4), 756-767. doi:10.1037/0022-3514.85.4.756
- Vallerand, R. J., & Houlfort, N. (2003). Passion at work: Toward a new conceptualization. In S. W. Gilliland, D. D. Steiner, & D. P. Skarlicki (Eds.), Research in social issues in management: The justice and fairness in the workplace (Vol. 1, pp. 175-204). Information Age Publishing.

Chapter 2

- Emmons, R. A. (2003). Personal goals, life meaning, and virtue: Wellsprings of a positive life. In C. L. M. Keyes & J. Haidt (Eds.), Flourishing: Positive psychology and the life well-lived (pp. 105-128). American Psychological Association.
- Locke, E. A., & Latham, G. P. (2006). New directions in goal-setting theory. Current Directions in Psychological Science, 15(5), 265-268.
- Relevant. Cambridge Dictionary. (n.d.). https://dictionary.cambridge.org/dictionary/english/relevant

- Sheldon, K. M., & Elliot, A. J. (1998). Not all personal goals are personal: Comparing autonomous and controlled reasons for goals as predictors of effort and attainment. Personality and Social Psychology Bulletin, 24(5), 546-557.

Chapter 3

- Dweck, C. S. (2009). Mindsets: Developing talent through a growth mindset. Olympic Coach, 21(1), 4-7.
- Dweck, C. S. (2006). Mindset: The new psychology of success. Random House.

Review Page

- Meraz, Remy. "30 Stand-up-for-yourself Quotes to Help You Take Charge of Your Own Future." Zella Life: Closing the Development Gap for Diverse Talent & Middle Management. Last modified March 16, 2023. https://www.zellalife.com/blog/30-stand-up-for-yourself-quotes-to-help-you-take-charge-of-your-own-future/.

Chapter 4

- Chong, J. (2021, February 26). Caught in the perfectionism-procrastination loop?. The Skill Collective. https://theskillcollective.com/blog/perfectionism-procrastination
- Flett, G. L., Blankstein, K. R., Hewitt, P. L., & Koledin, S. (1992). Components of perfectionism and procrastination in college students. Social Behavior and Personality: an international journal, 20(2), 85-94.

- Haupt, R. L., & Shockley, A. J. (2018). Ethically speaking: Analysis paralysis. URSI Radio Science Bulletin, 2018(366), 23-2

- Kurien, R., Paila, A. R., & Nagendra, A. (2014). Application of paralysis analysis syndrome in customer decision making. Procedia Economics and Finance, 11, 323-334

- Perfectionism. Cambridge Dictionary. (n.d.). https://dictionary.cambridge.org/dictionary/english/perfectionism

- Villanueva, M. T. (2011). Good things don't come to those who watchfully wait. Nature Reviews Clinical Oncology, 8(7), 386-386.

Chapter 5

- Miller, K. (2020). Positive Psychology. 5 Ways to Develop Grit & Resilience. Positive Psychology. https://positivepsychology.com/5-ways-develop-grit-resilience/

- Lee, K. S., and Robyn Smith. "EHR/EMR: "Meaningful Use," Stimulus Money, and the Serenity Prayer." Ear, Nose, & Throat Journal, 2011, https://doi.org/10.1177/014556131109000215.

Chapter 6

- Estapé, M. R., & Sánchez-Ocaña, T. (2021). Encuentra tu persona vitamina. Espasa
- Lee, D. S., Ybarra, O., Gonzalez, R., & Ellsworth, P. (2018). I-through-we: How supportive social relationships facilitate personal growth. Personality and Social Psychology Bulletin, 44(1), 37-48.

- Metros, S. E., & Yang, C. (2006). The importance of mentors. Cultivating Careers

Chapter 7

- Brown, K. W., & Ryan, R. M. (2003). The benefits of being present: Mindfulness and its role in psychological well-being. Journal of Personality and Social Psychology, 84(4), 822-848.
- Chambers, R., Gullone, E., & Allen, N. B. (2009). Mindful emotion regulation: An integrative review. Clinical Psychology Review, 29(6), 560-572.
- Covey, S. R. (2004). The 7 habits of highly effective people: Restoring the character ethic ([Rev. ed.].). Free Press.
- Hofmann, S. G., Sawyer, A. T., Witt, A. A., & Oh, D. (2010). The effect of mindfulness-based therapy on anxiety and depression: A meta-analytic review. Journal of Consulting and Clinical Psychology, 78(2), 169-183.
- Kabat-Zinn, J. (1982). An outpatient program in behavioral medicine for chronic pain patients based on the practice of mindfulness meditation: Theoretical considerations and preliminary results. General Hospital Psychiatry, 4(1), 33-47.
- Khoury, B., Lecomte, T., Fortin, G., Masse, M., Therien, P., Bouchard, V., ... & Hofmann, S. G. (2013). Mindfulness-based therapy: A comprehensive meta-analysis. Clinical Psychology Review, 33(6), 763-771.
- Keng, S. L., Smoski, M. J., & Robins, C. J. (2011). Effects of mindfulness on psychological health: A review of empirical studies. Clinical Psychology Review, 31(6), 1041-1056.
- Tang, Y. Y., Ma, Y., Wang, J., Fan, Y., Feng, S., Lu, Q., ... & Posner, M. I. (2007). Short-term meditation training improves

attention and self-regulation. Proceedings of the National Academy of Sciences, 104(43), 17152-17156.

- Veehof, M. M., Oskam, M. J., Schreurs, K. M., & Bohlmeijer, E. T. (2016). Acceptance-based interventions for the treatment of chronic pain: A systematic review and meta-analysis. Pain, 157(4).

Made in the USA
Las Vegas, NV
26 November 2024

12665053R00095